Beauchamp Library

4433

DATE DUE

DB M25/9		

Tanzania: My Country As I See It

Peter E. Temu

authorHOUSE

AuthorHouse™
1663 Liberty Drive
Bloomington, IN 47403
www.authorhouse.com
Phone: 1-800-839-8640

©2011 Peter E. Temu. All rights reserved.

No part of this book may be reproduced, stored in a retrieval system, or transmitted by any means without the written permission of the author.

First published by AuthorHouse   5/10/2011

ISBN: 978-1-4567-1430-7 (sc)
ISBN: 978-1-4567-1429-1 (e)

Printed in the United States of America

Any people depicted in stock imagery provided by Thinkstock are models, and such images are being used for illustrative purposes only.
Certain stock imagery © Thinkstock.

This book is printed on acid-free paper.

Because of the dynamic nature of the Internet, any Web addresses or links contained in this book may have changed since publication and may no longer be valid. The views expressed in this work are solely those of the author and do not necessarily reflect the views of the publisher, and the publisher hereby disclaims any responsibility for them.

Table of Contents

CHAPTER I: OVERALL PERSPECTIVE

How Poor Is Tanzania?	1
Is Tanzania All That Poor?	4
The Futility of Statistical Comparisons	7

CHAPTER II: DEVELOPMENT PRIORITIES

First Things First	9
Beyond Basic Needs	12
On Building a Vibrant Economy	15

CHAPTER III: FOOD AND AGRICULTURE

Agriculture: The Economy's Launching Pad	18
The Fight Against Hunger and Malnutrition	21
Towards Food Security	24

CHAPTER IV: INDUSTRY

Industrialization: Is Tanzania on the right track?	27
Putting industrialization back on track	30

CHAPTER V: SERVICES

Services: The Nation's Life Blood	33
Leadership: The Mother of All Services	36
Leadership at Managerial and Lower Levels	39

CHAPTER VI: TRAVEL AND TOURISM

The Value of Foreign Travel	42
The Limitations of Foreign Travel	45
Potentialities of Domestic Travel	48
Tanzania's Tourist Attractions	51
Enjoying Our Tourist Attractions	54

CHAPTER VII: FOREIGN AID

Foreign Aid: How It Helps and Hinders	57
Foreign Aid: Some Facts and Figures	60
The Key to Development is Trade, Not Aid	63

CHAPTER VIII: TANZANIA'S NATURAL RESOURCES

Land	66
Forests	69
Wild Life	72
Minerals	75
Water	78

CHAPTER IX: THE NATION'S BUILDING BLOCKS

Education	81
Health and Nutrition	84
Infrastructure	87
Political Stability	90
Law and Order	93

CHAPTER X: ASSORTED ARTICLES

Tanzania's Budget – Both Loud and Mute!	96
Loans: Using Other People's Money	99
Our Membership of the East African Community	102
China, Tanzania co-operation	105
The Sullivan Spirit: Building Bridges with Blacks in the Diaspora	108
Building for the Future	111
The Future Begins Today	114
Road Accidents – An Avoidable Disaster	117
Conferences: Expensive Talking Shops?	120
The Politics and Economics of the Oil Crisis	123
Is the World Financial Edifice About to Crumble?	126
Put a Smile on a Child's Lips	129
The City of Dar es Salaam and the Road Infrastructure	132
2009: Any New Year Resolutions?	134

FOREWORD

This book is an edited version of a series of articles originally published by the author under the title *'DR. TEMU'S VIEWPOINT'*. The articles featured regularly in the Monday edition of ***The Guardian*** during the period from January 2008 to March 2009.

The decision to compile and publish them as a book was largely prompted by the feedback received from the readers, both in Tanzania and in the diaspora. Recognizing that the presentations were of educational value, they suggested that they could be made permanently available and more widely disseminated if published in the form of a book.

The Author

CHAPTER I: OVERALL PERSPECTIVE

1. How Poor Is Tanzania?

Turn to any book or report on Tanzania published between now and the past ten, twenty, or thirty years: the chances are, there is a sentence – probably an opening sentence – which reads, "Tanzania is one of the poorest countries in the world". This assertion has become so fashionable, and is cited and recited with such an air of confidence and finality, that its truth seems no longer to be questioned.

In this and subsequent presentations, it is intended to challenge this assertion. It irks me to feel like we have all been brainwashed or hypnotised, and are no longer able to think for ourselves. It is as if the learned 'experts' from the Western world have decided to do all the thinking for us, and we have agreed to take their word entirely for granted.

The same experts have taught us appropriate vocabulary. They tell us that we are the victims of a 'vicious circle' of poverty – caught in a poverty 'trap'. The only way out of the trap, they say, is an external 'injection' of capital.

And to attract foreign capital, we must offer adequate *inducements,* such as tax holidays, repatriation of profits, and the like.

To us in the Third World, all this is familiar music. Tanzania has loyally danced to its tune ever since independence. Yet, the end of poverty is not in sight. We now say: 'enough is enough'!

Peter E. Temu

Together with fellow Tanzanians, we have to ponder the real nature of our problem, and explore possible ways to solve it.

But let me explode one myth right away: the myth that the solution to our problems will come from an external source. I am convinced that just as the source of our problem is internal, so must its solution be.

In the final analysis, everything rests with us: we must search our soul, discover the source of our problems, see what is needed to solve them, and do what it takes to rise to the challenge. Our resolve and our commitment is – we can do it, and we will.

In this introductory article, it is not my intention to dwell on any specific aspect of the Tanzanian economy. That is the agenda for subsequent presentations, which will entail a critical look at what is happening – or not happening – to various sectors of the economy.

Today's presentation has but a limited aim: first, to introduce myself to the reader; second, to lay bare from the outset my own personal convictions; and third, and most important, to invite the reader to join me in the debate regarding our country's economic challenges.

My own personal convictions stem from my lifelong experience in teaching, research and public service in Africa, plus 20 years in the international civil service. Add to this my constant thinking and reflection which have preoccupied my mind since I retired from United Nations service twelve years ago.

If you have read my opening remarks in this presentation you do not need to be told what my personal convictions are. My views are plain and transparent. I call a spade a spade. This will be my style throughout the book. It is a deliberately provocative posture, intended to stimulate thought and to elicit the readers' comments.

For instance, I am not a believer in foreign experts, least of all economic experts. Theirs is invariably a political agenda. Every time I see these people I know that their primary loyalty is not to Tanzania, nor to Africa, nor to the developing countries, but to themselves and the organizations they serve, or – what comes to the same thing – to the developed countries of the First World to which they belong. I make no apology for making such a blunt statement.

2. Is Tanzania All That Poor?

Tanzania may not be a rich country, but it is certainly not as poor as all that. Those who keep announcing that Tanzania is one of the "poorest" countries in the world must stop calling us names. I happen to know the world, and I know what I am talking about.

Admittedly, poverty is an economic 'disease'. It must first be properly diagnosed before a cure can be found. Prescriptions based on the wrong diagnosis only make things worse. Our first task, therefore, is to closely scrutinize the nature and extent of our poverty.

Poverty is a manifestation of our failure to satisfy basic needs. If we can overcome this stumbling block, we shall be well on our way to overcoming poverty.

We all know what our basic needs are: food, water, clothing and shelter in the first place; health, and education in the second place. These human requirements are normally met at the level of the family, the basic social unit. A family is counted as poor if it is unable to satisfy its basic needs; and rich if it is able to satisfy its basic needs (and much else).

As a believer in education and learning, I have no contempt for research or published works, official or academic. But forget, if you can, whatever you may have heard or read about poverty lines, per capita incomes, human development indices, and the like. Depend more, if you will, on "eye witness" accounts – based on direct observation – your own, as well as other peoples'.

Such is my own testimony – empirical, and based on my experience of thirty years of living and working in half a dozen countries, from very rich to very poor, on three continents – Africa, Europe and North America. I have also gleaned some useful insights from an even wider spectrum of countries across the globe where my visits, though short, have left an indelible mark on my mind.

Believe me, Tanzania is not all that poor. I have seen much poorer countries, and not just in Africa. Few, if any, Tanzanians need go to bed hungry.

Good soil and water availability (let alone good sunshine and fresh air) are far better here than in many richer countries. Why, then, are we not moving forward?

What Tanzania lacks are the resources and technology for food processing and preservation, and for eliminating pre-harvest and post-harvest food losses. We also lack the ability to handle crisis situations due to floods and droughts which, thank God, are not too frequent. Moreover, many of our people do not have the money or the knowledge to acquire the dietary supplements needed to improve their health.

Granted, our country is not prosperous – or not prosperous enough – due to a whole host of social and cultural factors, which put a lid on our progress. Our first priority must be to blow the lid off.

Once we do that, we can hope to achieve much higher living standards by mobilising our abundant natural resources – agricultural land, big lakes and river basins, beach attractions, forests and wild life and, above all, our vast treasure of mineral resources.

Admittedly, 'blowing the lid off' is easier said than done. Many of the socio-cultural factors which inhibit development and modernization are deeply rooted in our culture. These inhibitors operate at the grassroots level, and in a tribal setting.

Today, I want to highlight one such cultural inhibitor: witchcraft.

In Tanzania, witch hunting is not a metaphor but an actual and regular event. You will hear a prominent person say, as if in jest, that he is determined to settle scores with his adversary, "even if it means going to Bagamoyo"(infamous little town known for witchcraft). In one area of the country, a boy is abducted, dismembered, and his body parts eaten by a get-rich-quick aspirant; in another, an ageing old man is hacked to death by angry youths who believe he is a witch because his eyes are red!

I can think of nothing more inimical to progress than belief in witchcraft. In the entire history of mankind, no country in the world has ever developed economically or technologically on the basis of miracles performed by witch doctors. It is a fatal mistake that, instead of ruthlessly eradicating this culture, the Tanzanian leadership seems to look the other way.

As a result, there are numerous areas in Tanzania today where people dare not build good houses or establish modern businesses for fear of invoking the wrath and envy of the witch doctor next door. Mention a name like Bagamoyo, Pangani, Shinyanga, Mbeya, or Sumbawanga, and you instantly send a chill up people's spines!

3. The Futility of Statistical Comparisons

Poverty is a weighty issue, not to be lightly dismissed. Our ultimate goal is to increase our understanding of the nature of poverty and how to eradicate it.

For as long as this problem remains unsolved, we must go back to basics and re-visit the subject over and over again.

Poverty, it is said, is a wide concept that encompasses all critical elements which affect the well being of a person or nation. It is essential to distinguish between "income poverty" and "non-income poverty", their analytical components and statistical indicators which, combined, "provide a comprehensive, holistic picture of poverty".

Not all aspects of poverty are measurable and, furthermore, the non-measurable aspects of poverty are not necessarily the least important.

Poverty is an emotive word, which were better dropped from the international vocabulary. Applied to a country, the word "poor" (never mind "poorest") conjures up an image of thumb-print illiterates moving around with a begging bowl. Though purporting to be scientific, conventional statistical models are flawed because they are both foreign-oriented and culturally biased.

Of all the definitions of poverty, I found one that came closest to capturing the true spirit of the word. According to the Readers' Digest Great Encyclopaedic Dictionary, "poverty is a condition below that of comfortable living". This definition implies that a man is not poor if he is living comfortably. Conversely, anyone who is not living comfortably is poor, regardless of his status or material possessions.

The question then arises: what does it take to make a man, or the citizens of a country, comfortable?

We are now in an intellectual play field. Our new definition reminds us that poverty cannot be reckoned in terms of material things alone. It takes more – much more – than material goods to make one comfortable.

Unquantifiable as they are, non-measurable aspects of poverty are an important, if not a vital, component of human welfare.

It would seem, therefore, that a country's degree of poverty (or wealth) basically depends on two things: (a) the goods and services at its disposal, and (b) its capacity to enjoy them. Too often, international comparisons tend to overlook the latter, because neither human health nor spiritual or psychological wellbeing is amenable to statistical measurement.

The blunt truth is that no country in the world is as poor, or as rich, as portrayed by contemporary statistics. That is why I cannot cite, or accept, these statistics at their face value. Anyone who has visited these countries knows that the United States, Canada, Japan and Western Europe are not nearly as rich – nor are African, the Caribbean, and the Pacific countries nearly as poor – as the statistics make them appear. 'Comfortable living' and similar non-measurable criteria explain all the difference.

The hustle and bustle of life in New York, London, or Tokyo, the air pollution, the traffic noise, the incessant fear of terrorism, and much else that causes nerve-wrecking tension, anxiety, and stress – all this is a far cry from the tranquillity and peace of mind that prevail in many relatively poor rural settlements or city suburbs in Africa and elsewhere. If I had to choose between living in Tanzania, or living in one of these 'rich' countries, guess what my choice would be!

CHAPTER II: DEVELOPMENT PRIORITIES

1. First Things First

Whatever the task ahead, choosing one's priorities is always the first step towards orderly implementation. The task before us is eradicating poverty and accelerating development in Tanzania. How does one go about it?

In any free discussion, there could be as many views on a subject as there are participants. This need not bother us: indeed, that is what freedom of thought and expression is all about.

In the final analysis, when the views expressed have been weighed and distilled, consensus is likely to emerge. It is on that consensus that we must build, in charting our way forward.

I am convinced that this pragmatic approach, based on discussion and consensus, is preferable to any stereotype prescriptions.

Is there any consensus on what Tanzania's priorities should be?

I believe so.

In budgeting language, the term 'priorities' suggests an ordering of financial allocations by sector according to requirements. The same applies here, except that we are not concerned with just the allocation of financial resources, but with the direction in which our total national effort should be geared.

It seems to me that the top-most priority is the imperative need for honesty and integrity on the part of the nation's leaders. This is absolutely vital for 'nation building' – that old concept highly venerated by our early independence leaders. Without proper leadership at the apex, we shall break the nation, instead of building it. That is the stark truth. If I have not emphasized it enough, it is for want of vocabulary.

Next in importance, but still crucial, is the need for honesty and integrity of leadership at the executive level. This cadre consists of the executive heads of government ministries and departments, state-owned enterprises, and all major corporations, public and private, national and international.

These dual priorities underscore the role of leadership as the solid rock on which development in all sectors must be built.

At this juncture, Tanzania badly needs that 'solid rock'. Until we have it, a discussion of priorities is pointless; but once we have it, the remaining order of priorities for our national development falls easily into place.

National leaders of the first phase government, who were as far-sighted as they were dedicated, said that ours is a "war against poverty, ignorance and disease". They saw it as a three-pronged fight: there was little to choose as to which took precedence over the other. Their priorities were on a par; it was a war which had to be fought, and won, simultaneously on all three fronts. They were perfectly right, and it behoves us to respect those priorities.

Regrettably, to the contemporary Tanzanian leadership, fighting poverty, ignorance and disease has become a mere cliché – something everyone recites, but nobody seems to take seriously.

The result is the ethical deterioration and decadence that we are all witnessing. Unprecedented corruption scandals have caused Tanzanians to lose faith in their national leaders, whose call for poverty eradication is now seen as empty rhetoric.

If we can agree on the priorities, the rest is a matter of formulating policies and designing programmes for their implementation.

In other words: what, concretely, must we do to increase our production in agriculture, industry, energy, water supply, transport, and tourism in our war against poverty? What educational training, research, and technological dissemination programmes must we have in waging the war against ignorance? What must we do – or refrain from doing – in order to win the war against disease, and keep our bodies and minds strong and healthy?

This is no longer a list of priorities but a procedural agenda for their implementation.

The resources needed for implementation do not mean just financial resources, or even financial, physical and manpower resources combined, essential as these certainly are.

But there is one major resource which is intangible, and yet quite real, namely, a sense of commitment and dedication on the part of those who design and implement the programmes. Everyone involved – leaders and followers alike – must regard these as their own programmes, designed by themselves, for themselves; quite unlike 'mail-order prescriptions' from abroad which tend to be accepted, willy-nilly, as a parcel delivered by the 'experts'.

2. Beyond Basic Needs

Poverty eradication is the satisfaction of basic needs. But economic development, to which all countries aspire, goes way beyond that. You cannot think seriously about development, let alone do much about it, when you are weighed down by anxiety about where your next meal will come from.

That is why poverty eradication is naturally prior to development. Just as a man must be able to stand on his own feet before he can walk or run, so must people at the family level be able to 'make ends meet' before their national development efforts can bear fruit.

Earlier on, while discussing development-inhibiting factors, I singled out witchcraft as the villain of the piece. To this, I would now add poor health and the lack of education and training. These factors together tend to interact in mutual aggravation, and jointly militate against the war on poverty.

It is absolutely imperative for people, with state assistance if necessary, to ensure that good health standards are maintained, and minimum educational and training needs met.

It seems evident, therefore, that if the war against poverty is to be won, relentless efforts must be made simultaneously at the family level, at the level of the local community, and at the national level, in addressing the development-inhibiting factors.

History demonstrates that successful performance at any of these levels depends more on good leadership than on technology, financial resources, or any other single factor. Experience also confirms that in the absence of good leadership, even large injections of funds from the outside (including foreign expertise) will go to waste.

Once the basic needs have been met, the *development* task – what we euphemistically call 'nation building' – can begin in earnest.

What, then, is the way forward?

No one has the magic answer – not the government, not the myriad of so-called development agencies, not the learned professors, and certainly not this author. We should all as citizens feel free – perfectly free – to contribute to the debate as best we can.

The bottom line is that the development of our people, by our people, must have its own indigenous roots: it cannot be a mere transplant or carbon copy of some cherished model imported from the outside.

This does not mean, of course, that we have nothing to learn from the outside world. On the contrary, we have much to learn from the achievements of others, as well as from their failures.

Their achievements lie in the spheres of savings and investment, science and technology, modernization, the market economy, employment creation and income generation, and in their ability to plan for the future.

Their failures, on the other hand, normally stem from the excesses associated with these very achievements; and from criminal activity (such as money laundering) which typically accompanies development in this era of globalization.

It is pertinent to make a few observations on leadership and the fight against corruption, both of which are at the core of our country's development problems.

In Tanzania as in any other country, development has to be spearheaded by members of society with the right leadership qualities: those who have more than just the charismatic ability to make eloquent speeches and capture electoral votes; and who possess the honesty and the moral integrity to put national interests first and their own interests second.

At present, Tanzania is awash with huge corruption scandals – witness the ongoing saga about Richmond, Buswagi, and the Bank of Tanzania. Corruption on such a grand scale is crippling: not only does it slow down the country's development momentum, but it causes ordinary citizens to lose faith in their national leaders.

Unfortunately, too much lip-service and window-dressing still characterise our 'fight' against corruption. If the Prevention of Corruption Bureau, the official anti-corruption watchdog, is itself being alleged to be corrupt, Tanzania is truly up against impossible odds!

Forget the lack of investment funds. Forget the brain drain. Forget HIV/AIDS. Forget all development obstacles due to poverty, illiteracy, ill-health, lack of education, poor infrastructure, and the rest. *The blunt truth is that as long as corruption on the present scale continues, the country is doomed.*

What is required is a massive clean-up: a bold and merciless exercise, that will put the current leadership to a severe test.

3. On Building a Vibrant Economy

The Tanzanian economy – or any economy for that matter – is like a living body, composed of various organic parts.

Different economic sectors, such as agriculture, industry, mining, or transport correspond to different parts of the body. Various economic activities, including those which cut across sectors, correspond to the life-support systems which hold the body together and ensure its health and vitality.

It may be useful to keep this analogy in mind as we proceed, in this and subsequent presentations, to discuss the role of various economic sectors, and to study ways of building a vibrant economy in Tanzania.

First, consider agriculture - the much celebrated 'backbone' of the economy. The significance of the agricultural sector in Tanzania derives primarily from its overwhelmingly large size. The sector accounts for over 80 percent employment and 60 percent gross domestic product; produces food crops like maize, sorghum, pulses, cassava, oilseeds, rice, millet, sweet potatoes and wheat; and cash crops like coffee, cotton, cashew nuts, pyrethrum, sugar, tea, tobacco and sisal.

Most of our people are subsistence farmers or herdsmen, not by choice but of necessity. Land is their life blood. Apart from their own labour, and a few primitive tools, land is the only productive resource they have.

Unfortunately, the farmers' productivity is very low because they use traditional cultivation methods. They do not apply modern agricultural inputs, either because they are ignorant of them or are unable to afford them.

Year in and year out, farmers' fortunes are entirely at the mercy of the weather. Good rainfall means good harvests, poor rainfall poor harvests, and no rainfall means crop failure and possibly famine.

This depressing scenario may continue for decades, and could worsen, given growing population pressure and the predictable dangers of global warming.

Agricultural development in Tanzania is indeed a gigantic task. The time has come for us to 'take the bull by the horns'. Truly purposeful and aggressive action is a must.

A major shortcoming in our current approach to the improvement of the sector has been our comparative neglect of the peasant farmer. This is a grave mistake. At this juncture in the development of our country, the success or failure of our nation rests squarely with the small farmer.

What the peasant farmer needs is the motivation, the know-how, and the tools to do his job better. I suggest that the best way to motivate him is not by making lofty appeals to his sense of patriotism and nation building, but by re-kindling his own desire for self-improvement.

Charity begins at home. Simply teach the farmer how best he can help himself and his family, and show him what he stands to gain by adopting new technology and new farming techniques.

Encourage him to emulate the example of (and to work in collaboration with) his neighbour in the village, who is producing a better crop, or rearing a better breed of cattle, than his own.

Assure him that his neighbour's success is not due to magic or some religious miracle, but to harder work, superior knowledge, access to credit, better farming methods, better choice of seeds and fertiliser; along with tilling, planting, weeding, and harvesting at the right time.

Do not forget to add that his own lack of success is entirely due to his ignorance or lack of technical and financial resources, plus his failure to follow the rules of good husbandry. It is certainly not due to 'bad luck', or to bewitchment by an ill-wishing magician.

I am convinced that education and training at the grassroots level, oriented along such lines, holds the key to the solution of Tanzania's agricultural development problem.

Finally, we should not focus attention on farming alone, to the exclusion of other sectors. You recall our analogy of the human body? Crucial as it is, the agricultural sector is but one organ of the 'body economic'. While keeping one eye on it, we must keep the other eye on its reinforcing links with other sectors.

Our efforts at the farm level, if successful, will quickly yield surplus production, and with it will come the demand for storage, processing, fumigation, transportation, and marketing facilities. These in turn will lead to a series of new economic demands that will strengthen the growth and sustenance of the economy in general.

Success in agriculture, then, is bound to be a powerful stimulus for success in commerce, industry, and services.

CHAPTER III: FOOD AND AGRICULTURE

1. Agriculture: The Economy's Launching Pad

As you travel from country to country, or from city to city, in the developed world, you are often struck by what you see: big factories, extremely busy sea and air terminals, wide and well-lit tarmac roads, and thriving business centres downtown and in the cities' suburbs.

At first, the thought of how the country's agricultural economy is performing may not cross your mind; much less the realization that the successful performance of the agricultural sector is ultimately what lies behind, and makes possible, such advancement in industry, commerce and services.

Students of economic history recognize, and are always mindful of, the role of agriculture as the launching pad for economic development; much like a mature and successful young man always remembers and respects the role of his ageing parents.

This analogy is not far-fetched. Without the parent, the vibrant young man would not have made it; and without the good performance of the agricultural sector, the booming industrial, commercial and service sectors would not have prospered.

Turn now from the booming metropoles to the countryside. You will see large farms, using modern farm implements like tractors, combine harvesters and irrigation equipment; hybrid seeds, fertilisers and pesticides kept in on-farm storage facilities.

Beyond the farm manager, there will be a number of well-trained and well-paid farm workers. Agricultural productivity will be very high, and dependent not solely on rainfall but also on irrigation. Farmers would not be looked down upon: their income and social status would compare favourably with those of their fellow countrymen in the cities.

This is the picture of a typical advanced industrial economy in the developed world, which is what Tanzania, and other developing countries, ideally aspire to become.

But, in our admiration of the developed countries, and our legitimate aspiration to catch up with them, we have to stop and think: how exactly did these countries get to where they are? The truth is, their agricultural development came first.

All too often, well-meaning but untutored politicians, impressed by the glamour of big factories and commercial enterprises which they see in Europe and America, return to their homes in Africa and immediately recommend the establishment of similar enterprises.

Funds are solicited, and foreign entrepreneurs invited, but the resulting 'white elephants' (or 'ivory towers') which they establish prove to be a costly mistake. Far from being viable, these prestigious enterprises degenerate into loss-making national liabilities, and are eventually discredited and abandoned.

The lesson we learn from this scenario is that the development of the agricultural sector is the single most important pre-requisite for the growth and prosperity of commerce and industry.

If you travel the length and breadth of Tanzania, you will see numerous examples of failed industrial and commercial enterprises – textiles mills, fertilizer factories, meat processing plants, shoe manufactures, machine tools, etc. Some of these are being painfully resuscitated, with or without success.

In the rural areas the picture is even more pitiful. There has been little or no progress in the traditional cultivation methods used by the small farmer.

More than fifty years after Tanzania's independence, you still see people tilling the soil with hand hoes and cutlasses, collecting firewood and fetching water; plus poorly-dressed teenage boys (who should be in school) grazing cattle, sheep and goats.

Scattered over the entire landscape, as far as the eye can see, are traditional homesteads, usually thatch-roofed mud huts, with no water, electricity or fuel, only firewood and hurricane lamps.

This picture is typical not only of Tanzania but of much of rural Africa. Until it is drastically transformed, the agricultural sector will be a drag on, instead of a spearhead for, the country's development.

But can agricultural development truly serve as the economy's launching pad?

Emphatically, yes. This is the single most important point that needs to be hammered home.

The overriding fact is that the agricultural sector is so large (both in terms of population, output, and cultivated acreage) that even a modest increase in farm productivity, which cuts across the entire sector, makes a far greater impact on the economy as a whole, than would a proportionately much bigger increase in productivity in all the other sectors combined.

This argues in favour of making determined efforts to raise agricultural productivity across the board, knowing that it would have a tremendous impact on the economic fortunes of other sectors of the economy.

It also means that putting a lot of effort and resources into commerce and industry, while downplaying the agricultural sector, is so much misdirected effort. The development of the agricultural sector by raising farmers' incomes can and does make a big impact on the non-agricultural sector, but not the other way round.

2. The Fight Against Hunger and Malnutrition

"Food is more than just something to eat!" – said a radio announcement I heard while on a taxi ride from San Francisco to Stanford 30 years ago. The memory of this announcement came back vividly to my mind the moment I began to consider the all-important subject of hunger and malnutrition.

Hunger and malnutrition often go hand in hand. This is especially true where the problem is due to famine or food shortages. People who do not have enough to eat suffer from both under-nutrition and malnutrition; and, in extreme cases, the result is death by starvation.

For a proper understanding of our subject the distinction between under-nutrition and malnutrition is of the essence. Some people are malnourished, not because they lack food, but because they have poor feeding habits or do not eat enough of the right foods.

Sometimes people eat tasty and appetizing foods to the point of indulgence, forgetting the harm it can do to their bodies. The radio announcement I just quoted was targeted at American listeners, advising them to curb their appetite for palatable foods – the hamburgers, ice creams, milk chocolates, eggs, yoghurts, and the like.

In America, excessive consumption of such foods was believed to be the source of high cholesterol, obesity, diabetes and even heart disease. To drive the point home, the news media deliberately kept using derogatory terms to describe such foods, calling them *fast* foods, *junk* foods, or simply *junk*.

My point in making this little diversion may now be clear. Contrary to popular belief, the problem of hunger and malnutrition in the world cannot be laid wholly at poverty's door. Part of it is attributable to bad eating habits and poor nutritional education.

Under-nutrition stems directly from poverty, but malnutrition is due more to a lack of understanding of dietary requirements. Thus, though undoubtedly related, the two problems – and their solutions – are not necessarily identical.

The practical implications are two-fold. Among our national development goals, poverty eradication remains a major priority, and this underscores the need to increase agricultural food production. Boosting agricultural production in order to increase food availability was the topic of an earlier discussion, and remains part of our current debate.

The second implication is a recognition that diversification of production would be advisable, for the sake of the subsistence farmer's own nutritional health. In addition to the usual staple food crops such as maize, millet, wheat, rice, bananas, potatoes and cassava, a variety of fruits and vegetables should also be grown – and consumed – by the homesteads of rural families.

With a little effort and at no big cost, some valuable fruits and vegetables such as paw paws, oranges, cabbages, cucumbers, tomatoes, spinach, and egg plants, to say nothing of medicinal herbs, could be grown in the area surrounding the family residence.

The nutritional value of these food supplements can be substantial, not to mention the extra money income which can accrue from their sale. If adopted, these horticultural practices could go a long way to alleviating the problem of hunger and malnutrition.

Unfortunately, customs die hard. Subsistence farmers are known for conservatism, and it will take a major educational effort, together with well-designed practical demonstrations, to motivate them to abandon old customs and adopt new practices. Hopefully, persistence and perseverance on the part of the leadership will eventually pay off.

Another contributory factor to the solution of the food problem lies in our ability to stop, or reverse, the rural-to-urban exodus of young men and women. This internal migration of labour deprives the rural areas of a potential source of productive labour force, with no apparent compensating benefit. However, even if the urban centres have few or no job opportunities, it is mere wishful thinking to imagine that the labour migration trend could be reversed overnight. It will take some clearly tangible economic development in the rural areas to attract it back.

This brings us to our final point, namely, the relation between food security – which is what the fight against hunger and malnutrition seeks to achieve – and general economic development.

As a country develops, the industrial and services sectors far outgrow and overshadow the agricultural sector in importance. The availability of food, like that of any other commodity, then depends not so much on what is produced in the domestic market, as on the affordability of prices ruling in the global food market.

In a developed market economy, trade is what counts. All kinds of foods, processed and unprocessed, local and imported, compete in the food supermarket for the consumers' dollar. In a developed country hunger eradication is no longer an issue. Food is a comparatively small item of expenditure among a wide range of merchandise in the consumer's shopping basket.

3. Towards Food Security

Food is of vital importance to the welfare of mankind. If you want to bring a nation to its knees, deprive it of food!

By the same token, there is no greater source of comfort and confidence for a family than the assurance that a proper meal is available on the dining table at the right time.

That is what food security is all about. It is a goal towards which all humanity strives, and whose overriding priority is so obvious that it need hardly be stated.

The achievement of food security is a major step towards poverty eradication in Tanzania. For the subsistence farmer, food security is virtually synonymous with the size of his seasonal crop.

As crop harvest is itself largely dependent on rainfall, most farmers have come to believe that their fortunes are entirely at the mercy of the weather, and that there is little or nothing they can do about it.

This belief is false. There are many countries in the world with far worse rainfall, soil, and climatic conditions than ours, which have completely overcome their agricultural problems, enjoy perfect food security, and a high standard of living.

Moreover, food insecurity is not the result of crop failure alone. It is partly due to poor planning, plus a whole host of agricultural and cultural practices that cause pre-harvest and post-harvest food losses. With a little knowledge and foresight, these wasteful practices can be avoided.

No less important than food availability is the manner in which food is handled: the way it is harvested, transported, stored, processed, and prepared in the kitchen. All these activities – clearly a tall order beyond the scope of this presentation – impinge on food security in one way or another.

Tanzania – a tropical country just south of the Equator – is blessed with good rainfall. As is natural with climatic variations the world over, excesses do sometimes occur, alternating between droughts and floods. However, weather fluctuations in Tanzania are usually of modest proportions; extremes are rare and limited to a few localities.

Food security is perfectly attainable, if only Tanzania will rise to the challenge. It will take a commitment on our part to work harder, change some of our traditional practices, educate our farmers, and earmark a minimum of financial and technical resources for the purpose.

Our first priority must be to increase farm productivity. Practically every rural district in Tanzania has a certain amount of unutilised land suitable for cultivation. This is partly due to the toil of tilling the soil, which young men and women try to avoid by drifting to the towns in search of white-collar jobs, leaving their ageing parents and under-age siblings to do the 'dirty' work.

With no tractors or even ox ploughs, poor farmers using primitive tools like hand-hoes and cutlasses can probably cultivate no more than a half-acre plot for the annual crop. Untilled land soon reverts to bush, and is left for animals to graze in. In a good year a farmer may be able to produce enough food for his family, but in a poor crop year, his output is barely sufficient to keep body and soul together.

This scenario is typical not only of Tanzania, but also of much of rural Africa. Food insecurity in Africa is a perennial problem. Many good resolutions have been passed, but there is little concrete action.

This negative 'easier-said-than-done' mentality of self-resignation must now give way to the positive spirit of 'actions-speak-louder-than-words'. Our motto should be: we cannot afford to fail!.

How do we go about it?

In any rural community, there are always a few farmers who perform better than the rest. Once identified, such farmers must be made the nucleus of the community's leadership at the grass-roots level. Their role should be recognized and formalized through the creation of voluntary co-operatives. This co-operative effort could be given financial backing and technical assistance, and the farms made to serve as model demonstration plots for the rural community.

Where available and affordable, scientific cultivation methods, including the use of fertilisers, irrigation and hybrid-seed technology, must be applied to increase farm productivity on these demonstration plots. If widely adopted, such a programme could yield a considerable marketable surplus, sufficient to satisfy urban food demand and to generate the income necessary to purchase additional farm inputs, plus dietary supplements for the farmers' own consumption.

The purchase of farm inputs, and disposal of the marketable surplus, will strengthen the demand for various facilities, including transport and communications, thus stimulating economic growth even further.

Economic growth, by creating income and employment, is itself an important step towards food security. For city dwellers in particular, food security depends almost entirely on their ability to purchase from the open market the food and food supplements they need.

CHAPTER IV: INDUSTRY

1. Industrialization: Is Tanzania on the right track?

In everyday conversation, the expressions "industrialized countries" and "developed countries" tend to be used interchangeably, almost as if industrialization and development meant the same thing.

The pace at which a country's economy is developing can usefully be gauged by the performance of its industrial sector. In this presentation, we shall look at the kind of industrialization that is taking place in our country. Is Tanzania on the right track?

Here is a little story. A man longs to be rich – and to be seen to be rich – by owning a car, which he buys on credit. The car must be serviced, maintained, repaired, and eventually replaced; and the loan bears interest and must eventually be repaid. But at first none of these thoughts seems to bother him.

Within six months, the man realizes with the benefit of hindsight, that far from being richer, he is the poorer for owning the car.

This little story has a moral to it: it provides a cursory insight into some popular but misguided attitudes which may have influenced our country's approach to industrialization.

Tanzanians of my generation recall vividly the political euphoria and wild enthusiasm that greeted our country's transition to independence in the early nineteen sixties.

Understandably, the politicians had little time, and even less patience (never mind competence) to do the kind of cold, reasoned analysis that serious economic planning demands.

Long stigmatized as a poor colony, good only for the production of food and raw materials, Tanzania, on attaining independence, simply wanted to go industrial – and to be seen to go industrial.

The visualization was simplistic: developed countries were industrialized countries; Tanzania wanted to become a developed country; therefore industrialization was the way to go!

Not much thought was given as to which industries to establish, or as to whether such industries could be sustained in the long run. Once the political leadership had spoken, no opposition could be tolerated. Ahead went Tanzania with its industrialization policy (or lack of policy) without much hindrance of criticism.

Looking back, some 45 years on, can our industrialization be said to be on the right track?

This is not a question to be answered in the abstract. It requires a careful study of the manufacturing enterprises that actually exist, or have existed, in the country; plus an assessment of their present and future prospects.

In the space available, we can do no more than consider the types of questions which would be pertinent for such a study. Pose the right questions, and you are half the way to finding the answers.

Let us observe a few distinguishing features. Industry differs from agriculture in several respects. Firstly, industrial production depends almost entirely on man-made resources: plant and equipment, reliable fuel and power, plus inputs of raw materials. Secondly, it requires a wide variety of technical skills. Thirdly, it needs a well trained and disciplined labour force where each worker focuses on a specific task, performed in full co-operation with others: if a given worker fails to perform, an entire factory could grind to a halt.

So much for the production end, or the supply side. The demand side – entailing the marketing of the product – is equally important.

Is there a market for the goods produced? Who are the potential customers, and where are they located? Are there transport and communication facilities that enable customers to be reached and goods to be delivered? Above all, is the market price both affordable to the consumer and profitable enough to the producer?

The answers to these questions – and the list is not exhaustive – will determine whether or not our manufacturing industries are on the right track.

Without waiting for results from our research analysts, available evidence already suggests that all is not well. Can industrialization in Tanzania be said to be on the right track when so many of the industrial enterprises established over the years are either closed or operating below capacity? For example, in 1980, fifteen of Tanzania's major industries utilized only 45% of their productive capacity.

Here are a few illustrative cases of 'dead' industrial enterprises, with their locations shown in brackets: Ubungo farm implements (Dar es Salaam); meat processing plant (Kawe); fertilizer factory (Tanga); coffee curing factory (Moshi); textile factories (various locations); flour milling factories (various locations); petrol refinery (Dar es Salaam); machine tools (Kilimanjaro).

The circumstances leading to the demise or decline of such industries, and the envisaged remedies will form our next subject.

2. Putting industrialization back on track

A child's stunted growth, or premature death, can be scientifically explained, as well as the circumstances that could have prevented such an occurrence.

The same can be said of industrialization. The reasons that have led to stunted growth or to the premature death of our infant industries are not far to seek.

Even if the damage done cannot be undone, it is relatively easy to reach a consensus on how future mistakes can be avoided – in other words, how to put industrialization back on track.

Instead of dwelling on the merits and demerits of individual firms, we can take a more general approach. The intention is simply to highlight those factors or weaknesses in the industrialization of Tanzania which seem to be of broad relevance; and to see what lessons can be drawn that will enable us to avoid future pitfalls.

The principal weakness would seem to be that many of the industries established are out of tune with prevailing local realities. They lack indigenous roots, and rely excessively on foreign assistance.

Even if foreign funds and expertise were readily available – and they always come at a price – they should not be deployed without adequate involvement of local resources of labour, capital, and entrepreneurship.

Some projects require heavy initial investment, involving big plants and state-of-the-art technology, at a time when Tanzania may have neither the capital nor the trained manpower to make a meaningful contribution to them.

This has often provided the excuse for having 'turn-key' projects, which I regard as foreign transplants on Tanzanian soil that are of doubtful value.

A typical project in this category, in addition to its near-total reliance on foreign manpower, may continue for years to import the equipment it needs for repair, maintenance and renovation, on the pretext that no local product meets the required standards.

While the project retains a strong attachment to its 'parents' abroad, its links with the local economy remain weak or non-existent. The enterprise becomes a small foreign enclave, which makes minimal impact on the domestic economy.

Projects of this kind are undesirable because they provide little or no opportunity for the mobilization of local resources, whether in the form of capital, manpower or technology.

Advisedly, contractual arrangements made before such projects are launched should include provisions for the utilization of local resources, and the barring of unnecessary imports. They should also provide for manpower training at all levels, in order to ensure that, after an agreed initial period, the projects can be run successfully by Tanzanians themselves.

A crucial ingredient of local inputs commonly demanded by all manufacturing enterprises is the supply of utilities – electricity, gas, petrol, diesel, water and lubricants. For any project to be viable, regardless of who runs it, the availability of these inputs is essential.

Industrial projects established along the lines suggested here would seem to me to be on the right track, at least from the production point of view.

However, the viability of a project depends equally on the availability of a market for its product. While production for export is always an option, the hard fact is that as of now few Tanzanian manufactured products are competitive in the world market, whether in price or in quality. Tanzania's comparative advantage still lies with mineral products and with agricultural crops.

In short, for every industry that we establish, Tanzania's own internal demand must be relied upon to provide the market for its product, as well as the impetus for its expansion.

These observations cast a reflection on whether existing industries are, or are not, on track. They also imply what remedial action to take, where needed.

Is there an implicit lesson drawn from our discussion which could guide us to avoid future pitfalls?

Knowingly or by default, Tanzania did make certain mistakes in the past. Now we know better what to do, and what not to do.

One overriding lesson we have certainly learned: in setting up new industries we must be 'down to earth', not just metaphorically but literally. We should use <u>local</u> resources, establish close links with existing <u>local</u> industries, and try to satisfy (or prop up) <u>local</u> demand for whatever we produce. Yes, *"local"* is the keyword.

Import and export opportunities, and reliance on external assistance of any kind, must clearly take second place.

This implies that as our domestic economy grows, any industries we establish can be expected to grow with it, and vice versa. There will be no economic enclaves, no 'turn-key' projects, no 'ivory towers'.

Industry and agriculture will grow in step, giving rise to a healthy agro-industry which, in turn, will lead to the emergence of a vibrant services sector.

CHAPTER V: SERVICES

1. Services: The Nation's Life Blood

The services sector of the economy differs from other sectors in that it does not deliver tangible goods. But being all-pervasive, it is the nation's life blood.

Human welfare, if not human life itself, ultimately depends on the availability of services, and on the quality of services rendered.

A rough classification of the services sector may be in order. It falls under seven heads: infra-structure services; health services; educational and cultural services; financial services; legal, judicial, and security services; administrative services; and spiritual services.

Collectively, these services are the ultimate determinant of the welfare of society – be it a country, a local community, or the family unit. Human happiness depends as much on them as on the possession of material goods. Should there be a conspicuous lack of one or more of these services, no amount of material wealth can make up for it.

The effective delivery of infra-structure services depends on the availability of a good and affordable transport and communications system. There is no need to labour the point: everybody knows what a difference such a system – or its absence – can make to the economic and social welfare of the community.

Today's state-of-the-art communications transcend the boundaries of old-style posts and telegraphs, press, radio and television. Digital technology and the internet have opened up entirely new horizons, bringing the 'global village' closer to reality than ever before.

Health and medical services are necessary for the building, repair and maintenance of the human body; while educational and cultural services both inculcate knowledge and mould the human character. Between them, the availability of these services ensures that man grows to a healthy maturity, in body and mind. That is what enables him to live happily within his national and global community – fully energized, and confident in himself and in the world around him.

Financial services; legal, judicial and security services; and administrative services – all these serve to lubricate and hold together the entire social fabric, enabling it to deliver goods and services efficiently, and in accordance with accepted standards and norms of behaviour.

Last but not least, spiritual services. Essentially religious, spiritual services underscore the need – indeed the imperative necessity – to uphold a universal code of moral ethics in our daily lives.

Regardless of our religious persuasion, and even for those who profess to be atheists, everybody recognizes the importance of spiritual values, and the harm to society which the erosion of those values entails.

To Christians and Jews, this moral code is encapsulated in the Ten Commandments, the first three of which define man's relationship with God, while the remaining seven define man's relationship with one another. It is said that there is no religion on earth which contradicts the Ten Commandments.

One way to visualize the importance of the services sector is by imagining the dire consequences that would result from the disappearance of any given service. Pick any service at random, and ask yourself: "What would befall society if this particular service suddenly vanished?" Then extend the idea to the entire services sector!!

The services sector therefore acts, in one sense, as the binding force that holds together the various parts of the economy, and, in another, as the fuel or lubricant that enables the economy to function smoothly, harmoniously and efficiently.

Just for illustration, consider the agro-industry sector of the economy. As its name implies, this sector symbolizes a healthy marriage between agriculture and industry.

Their mutual 'love' is cemented by nothing other than the ready availability of services: economic services, such as transport and communications; financial services such as banking and insurance; and educational services on the application of science and technology to agro-industrial manufacturing processes.

The biggest merit of agro-industry is its ability to stimulate growth simultaneously in both industry and agriculture, making the two sectors mutually complementary.

This is possible because agro-industry relies primarily on the domestic market: it uses local farm products as raw material inputs for its factories; relies on local infrastructure services for both its inputs and outputs; and depends on the local market as an outlet for its products. These local roots enable it to become largely self-sustaining.

For that reason, agro-industry and its supporting services are a reliable generator of income and employment, and a natural step in the transition from an agricultural to an industrial economy.

This presentation has focused on the availability of various services, taking their quality for granted. We shall now consider the quality aspect, beginning with leadership.

2. Leadership: The Mother of All Services

In our last discussion of the services sector, little or nothing was said about the quality of the services rendered. It was tacitly assumed that the services were of adequately good quality.

We shall now relax this assumption. We know that the quality of services differ a great deal from country to country, within countries, and between sectors.

In Tanzania, there are some places which are totally inaccessible by road; and others where health services leave much to be desired, because hospitals, dispensaries, or heath centres are either unavailable or of very poor quality.

In fact, there are big shortages in just about every service sector you may think of. The reason is understandable: the country does not yet have enough resources to satisfy the people's needs.

That alone is reason enough why available services should be used with the greatest care, for the benefit of the majority of the population – and more especially, for the benefit of those who, through no fault of their own, are disadvantaged in one way or another.

Our society needs enlightened and dedicated leaders at every level – at the national level certainly, but at lower levels too. We need leaders who are incorruptible, who are altruistic rather than selfish, and who have sympathy and compassion for others.

When its top political echelon is occupied by leaders of the highest calibre and integrity, a nation has reason to be proud. By its example, leadership becomes a standing inspiration and a powerful force exerting a positive influence on all sectors of the economy.

Leadership assumes its rightful role as the mother of all services!

Unfortunately, leaders of such calibre and integrity anywhere in the world are few and far between; and Tanzania's case is no exception. Sadly, some of our leaders have succumbed to get-rich-quick temptations of the worst kind.

The 'list of shame' associated with the Richmond and the Bank of Tanzania corruption scandals, to say nothing of scandals in the mineral resources and other sectors, is ample proof that poor leadership is a major stumbling block to development in Tanzania.

Admittedly, it is not petty corruption so much as grand corruption that is the villain of the piece.

Petty corruption is a daily occurrence, usually born of hunger and poverty. Most communities yield to it, willy-nilly, as part of the culture.

Not that petty corruption should be condoned, or encouraged; far from it. It is a nuisance, and an irritant, but never a disaster. Indeed, under the forces of modernization and economic competition, petty corruption can be expected to wither away, and die a natural death.

Not so with grand corruption!

For one thing, grand corruption is confined to the nation's top leadership plus the leadership of big local and foreign businesses – and, at times, even foreign governments and international agencies.

Grand corruption is motivated purely by the lust for wealth by persons who are already well-off, but who decide to take advantage of their privileged position to amass huge fortunes for themselves, at the expense of the rest of society.

Unfortunately, the lust for riches is a monster that feeds on itself. Insatiable greed for wealth accumulation makes grand corruption particularly dangerous. It becomes a malpractice that never fades away: left to itself, it is destined to grow rather than disappear.

Based on this diagnosis, the cure for grand corruption seems clear. Obviously, no palliative or cosmetic treatment – in fact nothing short of total eradication – of this 'disease' will do.

Grand corruption deserves zero tolerance: it must be attacked frontally, mercilessly. Half-hearted measures are worse than useless.

The culprits are already in possession of so much stolen wealth that, given the chance, they can easily pervert the course of justice by lining the pockets of those charged with handling their cases. Parting with a few billion shillings in bribery is nothing to them, if that is what it takes to save their own skin.

In other words, unless these culprits are promptly apprehended, jailed and all their assets confiscated, there is a distinct risk that while their cases are 'still under investigation', we shall unwittingly have compounded the problem by breeding a new generation of corrupt officials!

In this presentation, I have deliberately concentrated on the top leadership, in order to highlight the harm likely to flow from Tanzania's on-going corruption scandals, and the need to take swift and stern remedial action. One cannot emphasize too much that corruption at the top level, if tolerated, may soon paralyse the efficient delivery of services throughout the country.

That said, we need to recognize that leadership at managerial and lower levels is important too. To this we shall now turn.

3. Leadership at Managerial and Lower Levels

Whenever we talk of national leadership, we normally think of the people heading the party and state organs.

A full appreciation of the role that leadership plays in national development, however, requires that we give the concept a wider interpretation. Think of leadership as a hierarchy – a pyramid, standing on a broad base.

It is the base that supports the top leadership, and not the other way round. Try to stand the pyramid on its head, and it will fall.

Thus, while one recognizes the crucial role of top leadership, one must not forget or underrate the significance of leadership lower down.

Leaders go under various labels. In the national political hierarchy, a president or prime minister sits at the apex, followed by ministers, deputy ministers, permanent secretaries, directors, and so forth.

In the corporate world, the Managing Director comes top, followed by department directors, section heads, and supervisors.

Churches have hierarchies too, with the pope or archbishop at the top, followed by cardinals, parish priests, and evangelists.

These examples have one thing in common: no matter where in the hierarchy one may be located, there is a leader at that level. It matters little what we call him or her; that is simply nomenclature, appropriate for the office.

If we are interested in the efficient performance of an entity, be it as large as an entire country, or as small as a municipality, and irrespective of whether the entity is public or private, our focus is invariably on the way leadership is exercised at each level.

It is axiomatic that there are no leaders without followers. Good followers are those who are both dedicated to their work and are loyal to the leadership. Good leaders are those who understand the nature of their mission, explain it to their followers, and are able to foster team spirit and at the same time recognize individual talent.

The bottom line is that everybody counts. Each individual has a role to play - a role which, however small, makes a difference. A mission is fulfilled when each worker plays his part.

In the ideal case, all actors - leaders included - work together creatively and harmoniously as a team, each giving of his best, and each receiving his just reward.

Under such an ideal scenario, the economy becomes vibrant, with all the good qualities: high productivity, brisk and profitable business, high employment, attractive remuneration, and a good source of tax revenues.

How does Tanzania measure up to this ideal?

Not too well, unfortunately. Of the shortcomings in the top leadership, enough has already been said in my past presentation.

Our current focus is on the next level of leadership. It consists of highly trained and experienced professionals in management and administration, in academics, and in scientific and technological fields of all kinds.

This is leadership at the executive level – a broad category where knowledge as well as commitment are of the essence.

Knowledge, of course, implies training and research; whereas commitment implies a life-long devotion to one's career. Both are invaluable; they need to be recognized and respected, honoured and protected, by every development-oriented society.

Regrettably, Tanzania's record in this regard leaves much to be desired. Resources devoted to research and training are clearly inadequate. What is worse, many Tanzanians who attain high professional and technical qualifications end up working abroad.

Why does this 'intellectual cream' of Tanzanians consisting of high-level scientists, medical professors, mathematicians, and state-of-the-art experts in information technology go to Europe and America, at a time when their skills are sorely needed in their home countries?

Admittedly, the 'brain drain' is not a uniquely Tanzanian phenomenon. It is evident throughout Africa and beyond. But given good leadership, Tanzania is perfectly capable of rising above this challenge, and showing Africa the way.

If we want to attract our sons and daughters back to Africa, we need to understand why they left in the first place. It is naïve to think that they left out of selfishness or for lack of patriotism. The huge remittances they make annually to their home countries, and their frequent re-visits, speak volumes of their loyalty and patriotism.

Actually, the fault lies with the domestic policies of our own governments. To the proud politician, this admission may be a bitter pill to swallow. But the undeniable fact is that we have not given our sons and daughters who work abroad due recognition for what their talents are worth, and offered them appropriate remuneration and fringe benefits.

These are not privileges but simply what they are worth and rightly deserve.

If Tanzania can move in that direction, it will have set an example of true leadership, and shown the way to the rest of Africa. But so far, it has not.

CHAPTER VI: TRAVEL AND TOURISM

1. The Value of Foreign Travel

Unless you travel the world, you will never really get to know what the world is like. Despite certain limitations, foreign travel has a value that is impossible to exaggerate.

Firstly, foreign travel is highly inspirational. It reveals to the human mind the wonders of creation as nothing else could.

As we travel from place to place, we see for ourselves, in all its grandeur and magnificence, what a wonderful creation the world is. It is an experience that is humbling to the human spirit.

Secondly, foreign travel has a unique cultural and educational value. It exposes one to a rich variety of cultures and civilizations; and shows how men, and man in society, are at once so different, and yet so similar.

Thirdly, foreign travel opens up new horizons in every field, offering both challenges and opportunities, and indicating how people in different societies, at different times, have confronted the challenges and seized the opportunities.

In short, foreign travel is truly an eye opener. You do not have to be a globe trotter to appreciate this. Any casual traveller who has had occasion to visit a limited number of countries, in different parts of the world, can readily attest to this.

To be able to adequately enjoy the fruits of foreign travel, prior knowledge of geography and a familiarity with one or more foreign languages are a distinct advantage. The educated tourist knows the map of the world, and understands the difference between equatorial, tropical, temperate and alpine climates. Changes in seasons and time zones as he moves from country to country come to him as no surprise.

Also to be expected and anticipated are the various geographical features over his travel route, which he will no doubt have read or heard about: big rivers, lakes, seas and oceans; snow-capped mountains and mountain ranges; equatorial forests, tropical grasslands, deserts and semi-deserts.

Travelling from Africa for the first time in 1967, and living for three years in the United States of America, I found the alternation of snow and bitter cold during the winter, and scorching heat during the summer – both of which I had anticipated – a thrilling experience!

The marvels of nature on the planet do not stop at its wonderful geographical scenery, which are peculiar to each country, and to each continent. They extend to the kingdom of wild life, from the biggest and most ferocious of wild beasts, to reptiles, birds and insects, to say nothing of marine life.

The rich abundance of Mother Nature is literally infinite. There is no end to the pleasure and enjoyment that a traveller can have as he traverses the earth across countries, continents, and over international waters.

But the world traveller is attracted by much more than just the unique beauty of the geographical scenery of the places he visits.

No less important, he is fascinated by the inhabitants of each country, who are foreign to him, and to whom he is himself a foreigner. Initially, a foreigner, even a child, will always attract attention, and be viewed as an object of curiosity.

Foreign travel makes human contact possible between the inhabitants of different countries. It is the beginning of experience sharing, of dialogue and, at official level, the establishment of trade, cultural, and diplomatic ties.

Contacts with foreigners uncover both differences and similarities. Wise men are able to capitalize on both.

Differences normally include both race and language, and the cultural practices that these underlie. But far from generating friction and misunderstanding, these natural differences, if viewed with humility and understanding, can be a source of learning and cultural enrichment.

Similarities offer even better opportunities. These are self-evident. Human anatomy, physiology, body chemistry, and much else, are all the same, regardless of race, colour, tribe or religion.

In one Shakespearean play, stressing this aspect of human likeness, the Jew says to his Christian adversary:

> "… *If you prick us, do we not bleed? If you tickle us, do we not laugh? If you poison us, do we not die…?*"

The realization that mankind is so similar in body and spirit, must have probably been the most important discovery of the ancient traveller when he first set foot on foreign soil.

By bringing together people of various cultures, histories, and civilizations, foreign travel coupled with various modes of communications have made rapid globalization possible.

As a special case, people also travel on pilgrimage, to see the holy places sacred to their particular religions. A Moslem visiting Mecca, or a Christian visiting Jerusalem, is an event of unique spiritual value to them.

Various world cities have become the cultural and commercial hub where different nationalities meet and live. The cosmopolitan populations of cities such as London, New York, and elsewhere, bear ample evidence of the impact made by foreigners.

2. The Limitations of Foreign Travel

Foreign travel is a good thing. But it does have its limitations.

To view the matter in perspective, one needs to know the purpose for which any given travel is being undertaken.

For convenience, we may classify foreign travel into two broad categories: first, travel for pleasure and recreation; and second, travel on mission, whether for public or private purposes.

Consider the latter first, and begin with African travel.

There is a certain asymmetry between Africans who travel to foreign countries (which I would call the 'outgoing traffic') and foreigners who travel to Africa (the 'incoming traffic').

The outgoing traffic consists preponderantly of people, usually young men and women of working age, going on mission of one kind or another. The purpose of their travel is usually to attend international conferences organized by governments, inter-governmental organizations, non-governmental organizations or, on occasion, business corporations.

Many of those travelling on mission are politicians or civil servants, students or academicians, businessmen or businesswomen; and a few are religious clerics.

With the possible exception of those travelling on private business, travellers in this category are typically on specifically designated assignments. Their travel costs and personal emoluments do not come out of their own pockets, but are paid for by institutional sponsors.

The sponsors' travel budgets, therefore, may be regarded as the main determinant of the size and composition of the outgoing traffic.

The opportunity to travel to foreign lands several times each year, at someone else's expense, is an inducement, and even a temptation, to people from relatively poor countries. Indeed, unless properly controlled, there is a danger that it may lead to wasteful expenditure of public funds.

This is the principal limitation or disadvantage of foreign travel by the outgoing traffic, a problem which does not apply in equal measure, if at all, to the incoming traffic. The limitation is virtually impossible to eliminate, given that the travel is financed almost entirely from outside sources.

Restrictions by an African government on its nationals travelling on the outgoing traffic would be viewed by many as an unfair denial of their travel privileges, which include entitlements to business or first class air travel, luxury hotel accommodations, sight-seeing opportunities, and per diem allowances much larger than their salaries!

The 'incoming traffic' is a different story. There are vastly more European, American or Japanese tourists coming to Africa than there are African tourists travelling in the opposite direction. This is because tourist travel is a luxury most Africans simply cannot afford.

By contrast, a large proportion of foreigners visiting Africa are fairly wealthy, elderly people, many of whom are pensioned retirees. These are tourists par excellence.

Foreigners who come on mission to attend conferences in Africa are comparatively few, for the good reason that most of the world's conference centres are located, not in Africa, but in Europe, America, Japan, and elsewhere in the developed world.

Because foreign travel is an important and growing industry, each country needs to exercise prudent caution, and reach a balanced judgement, on how best to utilise its scarce resources.

African countries, in particular, must carefully weigh the benefits of foreign travel against the benefits of spending an equivalent amount of time and resources in their home countries.

Even though the outgoing traffic is largely externally funded, it is imperative to weigh the benefit to the individual against the benefit to the community. An objective assessment suggests that it makes sense to reduce both the frequency of travel to international gatherings, as well as the size of delegations.

It must never be forgotten that every time the president, minister, or any high-level official, is away attending a conference or a seminar, a whole pile of unfinished business awaits them on their return.

Beyond the cost of travel, and far outweighing it in importance, are peace and security considerations. Not everyone who travels to a foreign country does so with clean motives. Some may be spies, terrorists, or drug traffickers.

Also on the dark side of foreign travel is forced travel, orchestrated by international criminals. Illegal immigration, and slave trafficking (including sex slaves), fall under this obnoxious category.

It is for this reason that the fulfilment of immigration requirements, including visas, passports, and physical inspection have long become routine mandatory procedures for international travellers. Enforcement of these procedures worldwide has become much more stringent since the horrendous terrorist tragedy inflicted on New York on September 11, 2001, in which nearly 3000 people lost their lives!

Unfortunately, perfectly necessary and understandable though they are, these additional travel restrictions are costly both to the taxpayer and to the travelling public.

International criminals have done irreparable harm to world tourism by increasing the risks and reducing the attractions of foreign travel.

3. Potentialities of Domestic Travel

Domestic travel, meaning travel within one's own country, may not sound as glamorous as foreign travel, but it is just as important and, in some cases, much more so.

To begin with, domestic travel is a lot cheaper. The distances covered are shorter, and there are no expenses incurred on visas and passports. All you need to do is plan your itinerary, buy your (much cheaper) tickets, and arrange your accommodation.

Regardless of whether one is a foreigner or a local resident, one is perfectly free to see the places and visit the people of one's choice; and to travel to any local destination with the available means of transport.

Domestic travel can be viewed from two different angles.

Firstly, it can be viewed in much the same way as foreign travel. Moving from one part of a country to another is not, after all, qualitatively different from moving from one country of the world to another. In either case, there is valuable experience to be gained.

Secondly, domestic travel has certain unique advantages, the most important of which is the spirit of love and patriotism that it fosters for one's own country.

Let us take each in turn.

From a tourism point of view, domestic travel can be just as valuable and interesting as foreign travel. It all depends on how attractive the landscape happens to be; and whether the country has any peculiar geographical features.

There are people in Tanzania who know a lot about foreign countries but who do not know their own country half as much. Many of them have only a fleeting impression of Tanzania's own tourist attractions.

They hear of places like Serengeti, Ngorongoro, Mount Kilimanjaro,

Mikumi, and many such sites, but they have never actually been there to enjoy them. This is true even of relatively well-off and well-educated Tanzanians, leave alone the poor and uneducated masses.

A deliberate effort deserves to be made to promote domestic tourism, by having special discount rates for Tanzanian nationals who go to national parks, and game reserves, and stay in tourist hotels. Tanzanians should not just serve as drivers, porters and tour guides; they ought themselves to form a major part of the tourist traffic.

Local tour operators, to maximize their profits, will probably find it to their advantage to re-orient their business, so as to cater not just for foreign tourists, as they do now, but for local tourists as well.

Another way of boosting domestic tourism is through a deliberate change in government policy regarding travel by its own employees. Public officials should be required to do more internal travel, and less external travel, than they do today; and that should form part of their official job performance evaluations.

Consistent with the new policy, the current gap between the privileges attached to foreign travel and those pertaining to domestic travel should be narrowed, if not entirely eliminated. The domestic travel record should count more than the external one towards promotions and salary increments.

As a matter of policy, foreign travel should be undertaken only when absolutely necessary. Whenever possible, fuller use should be made of teleconferencing and other modern means of communications.

The number of participants in inter-governmental conferences, particularly when held in countries where we have diplomatic representation, should be cut to a minimum.

The reason for this policy re-orientation away from external travel, and in favour of internal travel, needs to be made explicit. It lies entirely in the untapped political, social, economic and cultural potentialities inherent in domestic travel, which we have neglected for far too long.

Tanzania is a vast country, with a large admixture of tribes or ethnic groups, plus a rich variety of natural resources. Full familiarization with the country is necessary if we are to grapple effectively with the problems that confront the people.

Officials need to travel regularly from district to district across the length and breadth of the country, with their feet literally on the ground.

Travel should be by road, rail or boat, and seldom by air, except where access is impossible by any other means. During these familiarization tours, they should not skip inaccessible areas, just because they lack good roads, hotels or entertainment facilities.

Part of the officials' implicit mission is to meet and brush shoulders with their fellow countrymen who live in these locations, to learn of their problems first-hand, and hear from them what plans and aspirations they have for the future. If, in order to reach them, they must walk on foot, so be it!

Direct acquaintanceship with the people and their problems, within their own environment, is an invaluable experience. It is the first step towards the formulation of realistic policies that can be implemented with the people's active participation.

4. Tanzania's Tourist Attractions

This presentation takes stock of Tanzania's tourist attractions, while the next one examines what Tanzania must do to enable tourists to better enjoy those attractions.

Natural beauty is a God-given gift. Certain countries in the world are by nature well-endowed with tourist attractions but have not yet, for one reason or another, succeeded in tapping their tourist potential to the full. Tanzania is a case in point.

Other countries are far less well-endowed with tourist attractions, but through their own efforts, diligence, and imagination, have managed to create a high quality tourist environment. A good number of small or medium-sized countries in the developed world, plus some island countries, fall under this category. Tanzania needs to take a leaf from their experience.

The main tourist attractions for Tanzania lie in its beautiful geographic scenery, its national parks and game reserves and, not least, the traditional hospitality of its people.

Topping the list of our geographical blessings is, of course, the legendary Mount Kilimanjaro with its twin peaks – Kibo and Mawenzi. Permanently snow-capped, Kilimanjaro Mountain, the 'roof of Africa', captures the endless admiration of Tanzanians and foreigners alike.

One hates to imagine that 'global warming' might some day melt away this beautiful snow, leaving behind a huge rugged mound of bare earth. Tacitly, we may take consolation in the knowledge that we shall not be around to witness such a disaster, which – if it happens at all – is certainly many generations away! But we hope and pray that our descendants too may be spared such fate.

Other natural attractions include our water resources. Tanzania shares borders with eight different countries: Kenya, Uganda, Rwanda, Burundi, Congo Democratic Republic, Zambia, Malawi, and Mozambique.

The first thing that strikes one about the map of Tanzania is the way that water resources demarcate most of its boundaries with neighbouring countries. Three huge border lakes – Lake Victoria to the north, Lake Tanganyika to the west, and Lake Malawi to the south-west – have given the area international accreditation as 'The Great Lakes Region'.

The smaller lakes, on the other hand – Lake Natron, Lake Manyara, and Lake Eyasi – have one thing in common: they all lie within the Great Rift Valley, another distinctive feature of the region.

Finally, the entire eastern border of Tanzania consists of the Indian Ocean coastline, plus the offshore islands of Zanzibar and Pemba, all of which, in their own right, are famous for their beautiful beach resorts.

Next to our beautiful geographical landscape come our national parks and game reserves. Tanzania has 14 national parks and 17 game reserves; plus 50 game-controlled areas, a conservation area, two marine parks and two marine reserves.

Of all the national parks, the most spectacular are those located in the northern 'tourist circuit'. This includes Serengeti Park's vast grassy plains, home to over 100 different animal species, and world-famous as a wild game paradise. Ngorongoro Crater is another important attraction, in addition to Tarangire, Lake Manyara (home of the flamingoes) and Arusha.

The southern 'tourist circuit' has significant attractions too. They include the well-known Selous game reserve, the largest in Africa; plus the Mikumi, Udzungwa Mountains, Ruaha and Katavi national parks.

To the potential tourist, let me say this: it is one thing reading or viewing pictures of Tanzanian national and game parks, but quite another to actually be there to see for yourself.

The author can personally vouch for this. I recall vividly seeing the teeming wildlife as I looked down Ngorongoro Crater on my first visit there in 1974, just like I recall seeing Niagara Falls from the Canadian side for the first time in 1988. I had certainly heard about both tourist spots before. But actually seeing them was something else! How unforgettable!

Archeologists credit Tanzania with one more distinction: Olduvai Gorge, the 'Cradle of Mankind'. Located in eastern Serengeti in northern Tanzania within the Ngorongoro Conservation Area, Olduvai Gorge is a steep-sided 30-mile long and 195 feet deep ravine which is part of the Great Rift Valley. The gorge is situated on a series of fault lines which, after centuries of erosion, has revealed fossil remains of human ancestors 2.5 million years old, and a complete homo sapien skeleton, 17,000 years old.

A tourist is more than just a customer – he is a guest in the place he is visiting. Hospitality counts. If the feedback we have been receiving from visitors to Tanzania is anything to go by, we are confident that the cultural hospitality of our people is itself another tourism attraction.

The manager, receptionist, or tour guide at the resort centre does not only say 'thank you' when the visitor pays his bill, ready to leave. He will always smile, shake his hand, and say, *'karibu tena'* (welcome back).

5. Enjoying Our Tourist Attractions

We may now discuss briefly how to enable tourists, local as well as foreign, to enjoy Tanzania's tourist attractions.

The mention of *local* tourists should not raise eyebrows. Some people think, mistakenly, that a tourist is invariably a foreigner.

In fact tourism, like charity, begins at home. Each year, for example, more Americans visit the Grand Canyon, Niagara Falls, or Las Vegas than do foreign nationals; likewise, the largest number of visitors to the Riviera and the Mediterranean coast are not Asians or Americans, but the Europeans themselves.

If domestic tourism in an African country like Tanzania seems insignificant, the reason is perfectly understandable. At our present stage of development, tourism is still regarded by many as a luxury that we cannot afford. Travel for pleasure and recreation is not for people who can hardly make ends meet.

While domestic tourism may be expected to grow in step with rising incomes, our focus at the moment must be on how to boost foreign tourism.

The first thing we need to have is full and accurate information on existing tourist facilities. This should be made readily available, through our diplomatic and trade missions abroad, and more particularly to those countries with the largest number of potential tourists.

Appropriate preparations must begin in countries from which the tourists originate. Tanzanian diplomatic missions abroad should extend due courtesy to prospective tourists. They should ensure that existing visa and other travel formalities, as well as currency regulations, are facilitative, not inhibitive. Where improvements are needed, they must advise the Government accordingly.

Similar courtesies should be extended to the tourists on their arrival in

Tanzania, especially at their first point of entry – which is usually either Dar es Salaam or Kilimanjaro.

From the moment a tourist sets foot in our country, it behoves us to make good on our promises to him: open-arms hospitality, and sight-seeing and recreation facilities. Some of the tourists will be visiting Tanzania for the first time, and first impressions are always important!

The most serious inhibiting factor on the growth of tourism in Tanzania lies in transport and communications problems. How do the tourists get to Mount Kilimanjaro, Ngorongoro Crater, or Serengeti National Park, once they leave the airport terminal?

Our road system leaves much to be desired. There are only a few trunk roads radiating from Dar es Salaam to far-off border towns like Namanga, Mwanza, Kigoma, Makambaku and Mtwara, and not all these are tarmac roads. The roads leading to the game parks and other tourist resorts are of poor quality and often impassable in bad weather. Local tour operators often use light aircraft to ferry tourists to and from various tourist sites, but only the relatively well-off can afford this.

Without doubt, the single most important means of boosting tourism in Tanzania is to create a modern road transportation system that links the various tourist sites with the cities, and with each other. There should also be good travel links between the northern and southern 'tourism circuits'.

Moreover, every tourist centre must have clean and well-kept hotel facilities, including comfortable beds (equipped with mosquito nets), in addition to good food and drink, clean running water, and communication facilities.

Tourists take all this for granted. No tourist comes to Tanzania in order to enjoy a comfortable hotel bed or a swimming pool – there are enough of these facilities in his home country. The point, though, is that a lack of such facilities in our country for use by tourists would be enough to cut off the inflow of tourists. These ordinary facilities have extraordinary value!

There is also need to improve the country's security environment. We should tighten up security within the tourist zones, and hand out deterrent sentences to those who commit crimes against tourists.

No news is more distressing than hearing of a tourist who had been enjoying himself or herself on the beach, or in a game park, being robbed, molested, or killed by gangsters. Fortunately, such incidents are rare in Tanzania.

On the more positive side, there is need to sensitise the public on the virtues of tourism; on why it is in their own best interest to extend courtesy and hospitality to tourists.

A tourist is a traveller. Anything that improves travel safety is good for him. Regrettably, the poor quality of Tanzanian roads is only matched by the reckless driving of the bus drivers, and the virtual neglect by the traffic police of necessary road signs.

Everyone is dismayed that traffic accidents continue to take such a heavy toll. It is in the interest not only of tourists, but of all of us, that rigorous steps be taken to reduce road fatalities.

CHAPTER VII: FOREIGN AID

1. Foreign Aid: How It Helps and Hinders

No country in the world, not even the so-called super powers, can stand alone, either politically or economically.

On the political front, this is evidenced by the existence of a global diplomatic network, comprising embassies, high commissions, and consulates. Add to this all shades of bilateral and multilateral treaties, and the international relations fabric is complete.

On the economic front, similar links are manifested in international trade and finance, and the overwhelming predominance of the trans-national corporations; all of which signify growing global interdependence.

Foreign aid, the subject of our current presentation, cuts across both the political and the economic fronts, in addition to the military and philanthropic fields.

Except where there is an ulterior motive, foreign aid is something perfectly laudable and understandable.

But the caveat is all-important. Is foreign aid indeed ever altruistic? Might it be a mere concealment of the donors' thinly-veiled political agenda?

To answer these questions, we need to focus attention on three things: first, the countries to which aid is directed; second, the purpose for which it is given; and third, the amount of aid and the terms on which it is granted.

On each of these topics volumes could be written. In this presentation, we can only scratch the surface, though that is probably all we need to lay the truth bare.

Consider, first, the main aid recipients. It is clear at a glance that the largest amount of aid does not flow into those countries, nor is it used for those purposes, where it is most needed. The direction in which aid flows, the terms on which it is granted, and in what amounts, are all determined, not by the recipients, but primarily by the donors.

To put it bluntly, the donors' political and strategic interests are the principal aid determinants. Only on that basis is it possible to explain why, for example, far more American aid flows into the Middle East than into Sub-Saharan Africa; or why, within the Middle East (forgetting Iraq) far more aid goes to Israel and to Egypt than to all the other countries combined.

In principle – except for military aid – the same considerations govern the flow of multilateral aid as the flow of bilateral aid. After all, it is the same rich countries that largely finance the multilateral agencies like the World Bank and the IMF, that have veto power over how those agencies' funds are used.

Although much foreign aid is channelled through multilateral bodies, such as the United Nations and its specialised agencies, the constitution of those bodies, including their notorious veto systems, ensures that the poorer countries of the world (the aid seekers) are always at the mercy of the rich countries (the aid givers).

The inescapable conclusion is that foreign aid, by whatever name, always comes with political 'strings' attached. Even philanthropic aid is not entirely free from big-donor influence: that is why 'humanitarian' aid is not readily available to unpopular political regimes.

It is not my intention to try to discredit foreign aid – far from it. Given under proper conditions, and rightly used, no amount of external aid is too much. It is for perfectly good reasons that foreign aid continues to be solicited by one developing country after another as a complement to their meagre domestic resources.

But let the competitive bidders for foreign aid heed this warning: foreign aid always comes at a price!

Foreign aid agreements entail 'trade-offs', some explicit, others implicit. These trade-offs should neither be overlooked nor underrated.

What is the aid recipient expected to give in return for the aid he receives? The bottom line is a tacit expectation that the recipient should develop a sense of loyalty to the donor.

In the case of military aid, the natural expectation, which is sometimes made an explicit condition, is the forging of a military alliance. Civilian aid, on the other hand, including humanitarian aid, is expected to cement loyalty or a 'sense of gratitude' of the beneficiary to the benefactor.

When these expectations fail to materialize, the dark side of foreign aid rears its ugly head. Several unpleasant consequences may follow, including threats by donors to suspend aid disbursements or to cut it off altogether.

A donor-dependent country which is ill-prepared for such an eventuality, may be compelled to yield to the donors' demands on what it may or may not do, in such sensitive areas as human rights, good governance, and democracy.

Donor-driven demands of this kind are tantamount to blackmail, and are a clear encroachment on the dignity and sovereignty of the recipient states.

Public distress due to donor pressure is at its worst where the government budget is financed predominantly from foreign sources – a risk to be avoided at all costs.

2. Foreign Aid: Some Facts and Figures

We have seen that aid always comes at a price, and that it is important to understand what that price is. To see things in clearer perspective, let us beef up our narrative with some facts and figures. First, look at the global picture.

International aid falls into several categories: Official Development Assistance (ODA); humanitarian aid; military aid; etc. Even Foreign Direct Investment (FDI) may be construed, though cautiously, as a form of aid, to the extent that foreign investment is a 'win-win' deal, beneficial to both the foreign investor and the home country.

For illustrative purposes, we shall concentrate on ODA, and on the United States, both because of their paramount importance, and because their data are readily available.

The greatest providers of ODA are the 22 OECD countries, comprising Western Europe and North America, plus Japan, Australia and New Zealand. Between them, these countries, led by the United States, provided $58.3 billion in 2002.

Of this amount, the United States contributed $13.3 billion, followed by Japan with $9.3 billion.

Are these amounts large or small? They are large if placed beside contributions made by other donors, but small – pitifully small – if viewed against the needs of the recipient countries, and against what the donor countries themselves are potentially capable of giving.

The international community agreed long ago that a donor's contribution to ODA should be at least 0.7 per cent of its national income. Apparently, the decision was based on the 'ability to pay' criterion, a universal principle of equity, intended to ensure fair play among donors whenever a cost burden has to be shared. It was felt that any willing donor could painlessly part with 0.7 of 1 per cent of the national income without feeling the pinch!

This international yardstick enables us to lift the veil of selfishness and hypocrisy behind which some donors have been operating, and see them in their true colours.

As the US case amply demonstrates, the ability to donate is one thing, and the willingness to donate is quite another. Going by the evidence, the US is at once the most capable, and the least willing, donor country in the world.

Far from meeting the 0.7 per cent target, the US has been receding farther and farther from it, until it has now hit an all-time low of 0.13 per cent. This confirms that the US, the world's monolithic superpower, is by far the least committed country of the OECD donor community.

By contrast, ODA contributions by the Scandinavian countries, led by Denmark, Norway and Sweden, plus the Netherlands and Luxembourg, though smaller in absolute amount, are all past the 0.7 per cent target, signifying their greater commitment to helping the world's poorer nations.

Furthermore, a closer look at the picture reveals that well over one-quarter of all US aid is military aid directed at relatively few allies; and less than half is development or humanitarian aid; while the remainder (a little over one-quarter) is intended for 'political and security purposes'.

In 2004, only 18.3 per cent of America's total aid went to Africa (the continent of greatest need), compared to 36.4 per cent that went to the Middle East. Ten years earlier, in 1994, the disproportion was even greater, at 14.6 per cent and 57.8 per cent respectively.

These authentic figures, published by the US itself, are enough to vindicate my underlying message, namely, that any country in Africa which relies on foreign aid, particularly American aid, for the solution of its development problems, will get nowhere.

My contention is that a donor's generosity – or the lack of it – ought to be judged, not on the basis of what the donor hands out, but on the basis of the donor's unutilised capacity to give more.

US aid looks impressive to a poor country, but to the Americans back home it is mere chicken feed. What is a total of 13.3 billion dollars given as aid to the entire world by a country whose national income exceeds 13 trillion dollars, and which has an annual federal budget (forget state and city budgets) of $2.9 trillion?

Or, what is $13.3 billion compared to the $145 billion reserved for the 'global war on terror', or the $500 billion already spent (2008) on a fruitless war in Iraq?

From these facts and figures, one major conclusion is inescapable: we cannot – and must not – depend on foreign aid for development purposes.

Is Tanzania not risking too much in allowing its government development budget of 42.17 billion shillings to be 90 per cent dependent on the good will of foreigners?

3. The Key to Development is Trade, Not Aid

In the popular imagination, aid is a free gift, whereas trade entails payment. Does that mean that aid is better than trade?

Not if the goal is economic growth and development. It is trade, not aid, that holds the key to the economic development of a country.

The limitations of aid were discussed at length in my last two presentations. We saw that aid was usually given to meet a specific need, targeted to a specific group of people, and used under specific conditions. Aid also came on an ad hoc basis. Its amount, and the terms governing its use, were all donor-determined. The aid recipient had no option but to comply, on pain of aid being withheld, or future aid requests being denied.

These uncertainties and preconditions made it unwise, to say the least, for a country to plan the development of its economy on the basis of future aid expectations.

Trade, however, by its nature, is an entirely different matter, and opens up new horizons. In essence, a trading transaction is an exchange of goods (or services) between two parties. The fact that there may be one or more intermediaries to facilitate the transaction – by providing such services as storage, transportation, financing, insurance, and even a bureau of standards to guarantee the quality of the product – goes to show that trading activities require, as well as generate, a whole host of other activities that are of direct benefit to the economy.

But that is not all. Before goods and services can be traded, they must, of course, be produced, and in sufficient quantity and quality to meet the needs of the consumer. In a free market, this is ensured by competition among producers on the one hand, and between producers and consumers on the other, with the profit motive providing the engine that drives the market mechanism.

Finally, while trade is essentially an exchange of goods and services, the exchange process itself involves the use of money. In pre-historic times, people exchanged goods for goods, a process of barter. Today, people buy and sell for money, at prices determined by the market forces of supply and demand. This is another firm link between trade and the financial sector.

Trade, therefore, and foreign trade in particular, through its impact on the economy, differs substantially from foreign aid. Unlike aid recipients, trading partners are at liberty to make their own independent decisions, and the backward and forward linkages of their activities constitute a major stimulus to economic growth.

For all these reasons, it would appear that the superiority of trade over aid as an instrument of international development is beyond question.

This should send a clear message to the donor community. For what it is worth, their aid to the developing countries is only of limited value, and might even be harmful in the long run, by creating a donor-dependency syndrome. Regrettably, whether by design or by default, foreign aid in the contemporary world seems to be more in the interests of the donors than of the recipients.

The only exception concerns emergency aid and humanitarian aid, which will certainly continue to be needed. Ad hoc aid of this kind is meant to save lives, or to repair damage, rather than to build an economy. Any country which receives it must be sincerely thankful to the donor.

But development aid is quite a different matter. It is here that the world, led by the United Nations and its specialized agencies, needs to do some serious re-thinking.

Is international development aid really achieving its intended purpose? My viewpoint is that the resources used for this purpose would yield far better dividends if used instead to promote trade for the recipient countries. The impact on economic growth would be much greater and more sustainable.

Apparently, donor countries do not seem to realize that the benefit of their development aid is largely nullified by the damage done by their agricultural subsidies and other domestic policies which deny the recipients access to the donors' markets.

It is ironical that the same countries which maintain agricultural subsidies for their own farmers, want the developing countries to open up their markets to global competition. Giving financial aid to developing countries while at the same time denying them market access for their agricultural products is double standards. It only inhibits their growth and perpetuates their aid-dependent status.

The key to development is trade, not aid!

CHAPTER VIII: TANZANIA'S NATURAL RESOURCES

1. Land

Natural resources are part of God's creation and a worthy gift to mankind. Land, sunlight, air, water, animals and vegetation are not man-made, but God-given.

Long before the dawn of civilization, ancient man subsisted on hunting and fruit gathering. Millenniums later, man began to establish rural settlements, using primitive tools to till the soil and cultivate crops, and to rear animals .

Such were the early beginnings of agriculture and animal husbandry, which preceded the growth of commerce, industry, and urbanization.

Land, the mother of life on earth, holds and nurtures other natural resources, including oceans, lakes, minerals, and vegetation. Land not only gives succour to plant, animal, and human life, but also generously provides their final resting place. In what follows, we shall dwell mainly on agricultural land, ending with a few words on urban land.

Tanzania has no scarcity of agricultural land. Why, then, are we not free from food shortages? Ironically, the problem is not that there is too little land for agriculture, but too much!

'Shifting cultivation' reflects this reality. Many farmers do not cultivate the same piece of land each year. They do not adopt improved methods of crop husbandry and maintaining soil fertility.

Seeing that there is spare land available, the farmer's tendency is to abandon the plot he has cultivated this year, shift to another one the following year, and to yet another the year after that. He then returns to his original plot which, being fallow, will hopefully have recovered its natural fertility. Thus, he can repeat the cycle, without feeling the urge to change his farming methods.

A parallel practice is apparent with livestock farmers. Instead of confining his livestock to a small patch or enclosure, and rearing them intensively, the peasant farmer lets his animals drift and graze over a wide area, just because there seems to be so much land available.

Unfortunately, both shifting crop cultivation and shifting livestock grazing share two distinct disadvantages. Firstly, the practice encourages low-productivity subsistence farming – the classic way to perpetuate poverty. Secondly, with rising human and livestock populations, land scarcity soon manifests itself.

Crop cultivators and livestock grazers then find themselves pitted against each other, trading accusations for encroaching on each other's land. This often leads to violent clashes between farmers and pastoralists.

If all the land suitable for agriculture was properly cultivated, Tanzania would not only be self-sufficient in food, but could feed the rest of Africa; and if Africa would adopt scientific farming methods, she could feed the world.

But, why are we so far from this optimistic scenario, to the extent that many parts of our continent face hunger and starvation? One reason is the prevalence of political turmoil, rooted in poor leadership, personal greed, and the lust for power.

Look at Zimbabwe's political chaos and economic shambles. Look at DRC Congo, which has never known peace since the death of Patrice Lumumba nearly 60 years ago.

Look at Mauritannia, Chad, Ivory Coast, Sierra Leone, and Guinea Bissau. Look at Uganda's LRA, Sudan's Darfur, and Somalia's unending civil war and ship piracy.

Without peace and security, progress of any kind is a nightmare. Yet, the presence of peace and security alone is not enough, as Tanzania's case amply demonstrates. At least two more obstacles must be overcome. The first is the failure to embrace agricultural science and technology, and doing the necessary research. Tanzania, like the rest of Africa, has yet to modernize and transform its agriculture.
A campaign needs to be mounted to educate and motivate farmers, coupled with the effective mobilization of financial, technical, material and human resources. Appropriate rewards should be given to farmers who perform well, and penalties meted out to those who do not.

A necessary step is to institute changes in land tenure. Rural land surveys should be carried out, farmers registered, and ownership titles granted, exactly as is done for urban dwellers.

To ensure efficient land utilization, land titles could be bought, sold and, if necessary, revoked. Customary laws safeguarding traditional 'tribal land' and communal land tenure have long outlived their usefulness. As for urban land, an important measure would be to carry out surveys which will permit the registration of building plots at an early stage of urban growth.

Such early pre-planning would prevent the haphazard mushrooming of slums in urban areas, and their costly demolition when official surveys and plots registrations are eventually undertaken.

The second fundamental obstacle to development is the lack of honesty and integrity, giving rise to graft and corruption. Let us face it: corruption and the theft of public funds – on a scale that is typical of Nigeria, or that has been revealed in Tanzania's recent scandals– is a crippling blow to the development efforts of any country.

2. Forests

Natural resources, including forests, do not belong to private individuals but to the community as a whole, and are held by the state in custody for present and future generations.

Many urban dwellers, and even rural inhabitants, may live a whole lifetime without ever seeing a forest. Trees, grass, bushes, and vegetation of all kinds (which are a common sight to all of us) are one thing; but forests are something else.

To the environmental scientist, a forest has the same appeal or attraction that a tourist site has for a traveller. But to the ordinary man, his interest in forests is probably limited to particular forest products supplied by game hunters, wood hewers and fruit gatherers which he uses and enjoys.

The environmental research scientist is attracted by the rich diversity of animal, plant and insect species, for which forests are the natural habitat.

It is said that rainforests alone are home to half of the living plant and animal species on the planet. A major reason against the depletion or destruction of forests is that it destroys the natural environment of wild life, including some valuable rare species which are the object of world conservation efforts.

In recounting the benefits to be derived from forests, the first thing that comes to mind is forest products. Of these, probably the most familiar is timber. For construction and various installations, certain tree species are especially important, and are a useful, and much cheaper, substitute for metallic materials.

A common example is the use of timber in scaffolding for construction purposes, or as electric poles for purposes of 'transporting' electricity over long transmission lines across the country.

Where timber is readily available and can be properly cut, dried, and treated with insecticide, such timber can be quite durable and economical to use.

Another important use of forest timber is its utilisation for furniture purposes. We regularly use and admire the beauty of all kinds of carpentry products – wooden gates, doors, windows, shelves, tables, chairs, beds, and wooden floors and ceilings – to say nothing of pulp and paper products; and we sometimes forget that all these products originate from logging in the forests.

Forests remain a major source of natural, unprocessed foodstuffs. These include game meat, insects-originated nutrients such as honey, fruits and apples, plus some plant roots and herbs.

Many forest products also have medicinal value. Before the era of modern medicine, people relied extensively on medicinal roots, herbs, and tree barks to treat various ailments. Tropical rainforests have been called the 'world's largest pharmacy' because over one-quarter of modern medicines originate from its plants.

It might well be that one of the undiscovered secrets for the treatment of tropical diseases lies hidden in this tropical forest environment, whose huge 'pharmacy' still has much potential, waiting to be tapped by future researchers.

With population growth, reliance on these valuable forest products is on the increase. To cope with the increased demand, it is necessary to encourage planned tree planting and reforestation.

Apart from forest products, the reason why forests are such a valuable asset for humanity is because of their impact on the environment. For example, the equatorial rainforest around the globe is so called because it covers a geographical belt around the equator (which includes such countries as Congo in Africa and Brazil in Latin America), and is known both for its high rainfall and its thick forests.

As one moves longitudinally farther and farther away from the equator, one soon comes across the temperate zone forests, with coniferous and deciduous trees, including eucalyptus; and trees which are useful for plywood, as well as pulp and paper products.

Wherever they happen to be, forests are regarded as rain catchment areas; because they attract clouds and rainfall precipitation, keep the environment green, and support a rich variety of wild life.

Some parts of the world are naturally devoid of forests, notably the polar regions, the tropical deserts, and most of the savannah grassland region.

There are, however, large expanses of territory which were once under forest but which have now become deforested. Partly this has been due to sprawling urban development, but also to agricultural encroachment, reckless tree-felling and incidental forest fires.

In many African countries, including Tanzania, haphazard bush fires and the indiscriminate felling of trees for charcoal and firewood are contributing to environmental deterioration, semi-desertification, poor cloud formation, scattered rainfall, and the depletion of water sources.

The new public emphasis on forest conservation and environmental protection is therefore much to be commended. But it needs to go beyond urban landscaping, street cleaning, and symbolic tree-planting ceremonies, to entail proper reforestation, plus effective control of bush fires and random charcoal burning in the rural areas.

3. Wild Life

The sight of a wild animal is always a cause of excitement and curiosity. This is especially so where the animal is seen in its natural environment.

I have vivid memories of this experience from the time I was a child, probably aged 6 or 7. At that time, I used to graze my father's sheep and goats at Mwika Kimangaro, in what is now Kilimanjaro region, Moshi rural district, close to a valley known as Karango.

There, up a tree, a monkey could be seen jumping from branch to branch. Once, I tried to frighten it away by waving a twig, only to find myself scared stiff, as the animal would not budge, but instead kept staring at me defiantly with unblinking eyes.

Later, on hearing of this, my father said to me that no monkey will ever be scared away by the sight of a child or a woman. I find it remarkable that even now, at 72 years of age, my curiosity and fascination with wild life has not diminished; if anything, it has increased.

As I write, I find myself reflecting on the many opportunities still available for Tanzanian nationals, to enjoy the pleasures and excitement of wild life in our game reserves.

I used to think – as many people still do – that these facilities were there primarily for the enjoyment of foreign tourists. But now we know better. These game reserves, teeming with wild life, belong here, as part of our heritage. Foreigners pay millions of money to come and see them. But we Tanzanians, being already here, pay next to nothing. All the wild game is ours to enjoy!

Wild animals are scary, and even dangerous. Paradoxically, that is also the reason why seeing them is so exciting. As you get close to a wild animal, and focus your camera, your heart beat increases rapidly with fear and curiosity.

Many people who have seen a lion, a tiger, or a cobra at close range have probably seen them, not in their natural habitat, but in a zoo. Admittedly, it is less dangerous watching a lion 'behind bars', pacing impatiently back and forth as if looking for somebody to devoir, than seeing it on a rampage in the wilderness.

People best satisfy their pleasure when the wild animals, birds, reptiles or insects are viewed live in their natural habitat – in the forests, bushes, open plains, river banks, or wherever.

The next best thing is watching them in a zoo; and, last of all, watching them on video, or simply reading about them in books and magazines!

Beyond the self-satisfaction that one gets from game viewing, there is the wider benefit that accrues to the nation through its impact on tourism. It is for this reason that a government ministry exists for the dual purpose of protecting wild life and promoting tourism.

Natural resources, such as forests and wild life, cannot be regarded as the private property of any one individual or social entity. They are held by the state in trust for all its citizens, including future generations. That is why indiscriminate hunting (or poaching) of wild game, like the indiscriminate destruction of forests for private profit, is unlawful.

Poaching by unlicensed hunters deserves stiff penalties. Poachers kill elephants for their ivory tusks, while leopards and zebra are often hunted for their skins, and other animals for their meat. These are all products that can, and should, be obtained lawfully in properly constituted markets.

Viewed in a wider context, all natural resources, and wild life in particular, are the heritage of all mankind, irrespective of national boundaries. Any existing resource must, by definition, be located within the national boundaries of some particular country, but that is no reason why that country alone should have, or think it has, the sole right to it.

The world regrets that certain life species have become extinct, probably through human fault and neglect over past millenniums; and right now some endangered species are on the verge of extinction unless properly recognized and cared for. (Part of UNESCO's mandate is to identify and protect such species in the interest of humanity wherever they may be found on the planet).

Peter E. Temu

The growth of world tourism, based on the full potentialities of wild life management, is literally limitless. This potential is waiting to be tapped.

One way to do so would be for schools to organize game-viewing trips for their students once each year. This would strengthen their admiration of wild animals from an early age. It is anybody's guess what impact on global tourism this could have in later years when the children grow up to maturity!

4. Minerals

Unlike other natural resources, minerals lie hidden under the ground. Before a country can know whether or not there is mineral wealth beneath its soil – and what type of minerals – exploration is necessary.

If successful, mineral exploration is then followed by actual mining operations, which entail excavation to reach the mineral deposits, bringing them up to the surface, extracting the ore, and carrying out such further refinements as may be needed.

Mining is an expensive venture, fraught with uncertainty. It may take years of exploration to detect the presence (or confirm the absence) of mineral deposits.

Even after one or more minerals have been discovered, one must decide whether it pays to incur the cost of mining it. The answer will depend entirely on market conditions.

Mining can also be a highly lucrative activity if you are lucky enough to hit a bonanza. Usually, however, the process takes time; mining entrepreneurs will not become rich overnight.

A number of African countries have an impressive amount of mineral deposits: gold and diamonds in South Africa, copper in Zambia and Angola, gold in Ghana, Tanzania and DRC Congo, oil in Nigeria, Libya and Sudan. The list is not exhaustive. Yet, hardly any of these counties has risen far above the poverty line.

Hence the big question: why is Africa unable to shake off its poverty despite its mineral wealth? Why is it that oil-rich Nigeria, for instance, for many years a member of OPEC, is still counted as one of the least developed countries?

The same applies to other mineral-rich countries, for example Tanzania, which is well-known for its gold, diamonds and Tanzanite.

Another relevant question is why mineral discoveries make so little impact on the development of the country's economy. Any casual observer of the African scene can see that mining has not contributed to the national economy, or to the economy in the vicinity of the mines, anything commensurate with the value of the mining operations.

The reasons for this need to be carefully studied, if a realistic future policy is to be formulated. Let us not be quick to admit – nor quick to deny – that the blame is to be laid at the door of foreign exploiters. We need to analyse the evidence carefully before jumping to a conclusion.

Meanwhile, a few points are worth noting.

Firstly, precisely because mining is so costly, continued reliance on foreign assistance seems virtually unavoidable. Local residents can barely afford the cost of mineral exploration, let alone undertaking the actual mining operations.

Secondly, mining is also a highly skilled and capital-intensive enterprise. Even assuming that we could locally raise the money need, we would still continue to rely on foreign technical expertise for the foreseeable future.

Thirdly, precisely because foreign involvement is inevitable, skilful negotiation of foreign contracts is absolutely imperative. Contracts will be both country-specific and mineral-specific. The negotiations themselves will put the skills, integrity, and altruism of negotiators to the test.

Naturally, each side will try to strike the best deal for itself. If foreign negotiators take advantage of our technical ignorance, that will be our fault, not theirs. We need to be on our guard against any overstretched loopholes.

Typically, foreigners want a contract that contains a provision for 'tax holiday' for an initial period of, say, five to ten years, during which they can repatriate all their profits tax-free.

They may also require a guaranteed period of even up to thirty years or more during which they can continue to exploit the mining enterprise without any competition or interference from outside.

Usually, the contract will also include provision for the training of local personnel, as well as some formula for the sharing of profits between the government and the foreign investor after some specified initial period.

These contracts are normally subject to international arbitration in case of dispute, and they provide for stiff penalties on the government in cases of infringement or unilateral abrogation.

We are not on a level playfield. The relationship between the parties is clearly asymmetrical. The side seeking the mineral concessions is rich and powerful, and the one granting such concessions is poor, and lacking in technical expertise.

For these reasons, the negotiation of mining contracts in Africa are typically open to bribery and corruption; and must be handled with the highest honesty and integrity.

These considerations are not limited to the mineral sector. They apply equally to foreign contracts in the energy, transport and communications sectors.

It would appear that one way to avoid a repetition of past blunders would be to have a permanent team of well-trained professional contract negotiators. Consisting of legal and technical experts, the team would thoroughly scrutinize and approve each foreign contract before it is signed.

5. Water

Did you know that about 75 per cent of the human body consists of water? And that water covers 71 per cent of the earth's surface?

Like air and sunlight, water is a natural resource provided free by Nature to sustain life on earth. Without water, life as we know it is inconceivable.

Incidentally, it is the huge quantity of water, resting on the oceans, that gives most of our planet its distinctive blue appearance when viewed from outer space. The continued availability of water on the planet is assured, among other means, by the processes of evaporation, condensation and rainfall precipitation; and by the melting of snow from the polar ice caps.

If studied as a school subject, water would fill volumes in just about every discipline – science, geography, agriculture, medicine, you name it. A Christian could even claim: 'no water, no baptism'.

In what follows, attention is focused on water as an economic asset. It is pointed out that its inadequacy or misuse poses a serious threat both to our economic welfare and our human health.

Like all countries that depend on agriculture, Tanzania's economic fortunes are largely dependent on rain water. Good rains mean a bumper harvest, while poor rains or drought mean a harvest failure.

For those engaged in livestock grazing, good rains mean an abundance of good grass to feed their animals, while prolonged drought could starve them to death for lack of grass and drinking water.

Whether engaged in crop farming or in livestock grazing, the challenge is the same: farmers must find ways to ensure water availability at those times and places where rain water is lacking or inadequate.

In the absence of adequate knowledge and capital needed for irrigation, the only option for the peasant farmer is to migrate temporarily to new areas (if they exist) with better rainfall conditions. Failing this, he must seek famine relief, or starve to death.

Tanzania – a vast country – does have its wet and dry seasons, but the weather is never uniformly extreme throughout the year, or from one region to the next.

Moreover, the country is well endowed with natural water sources – rivers, lakes, and the long Indian Ocean coastline. If only these natural water sources could be properly tapped and used for irrigation, Tanzania would experience a dramatic increase in food supply, in addition to export crops, and improvements in animal husbandry.

These enormous irrigation potentialities have long been known, and are advocated repeatedly by government officials and by vote-seeking politicians. But the gap between actions and words remains wide.

As a cleaning agent, water is a hygienic necessity. It washes our bodies clean, and keeps them healthy. There is no substitute for the refreshingly warm (or cold) bath under the shower or in the bath tub.

Besides, we need water to wash our clothes, vehicles, house floors, kitchen utensils and all sorts of domestic and industrial appliances. Equally important, water is used for drainage purposes, for flushing toilets and for sewage disposal.

Across big rivers all over the world, water dams have been built, for two main commercial purposes – the generation of electric power, and the irrigation of agricultural land.

All these multifarious uses of water–and the list is not exhaustive–serve to underline the vital role of this important natural resource.

It is also a powerful reminder to us that in the interest of present and future generations, this natural asset must be preserved and protected, and must never be misused.

One way to prevent existing water sources, such as springs, wells, fountains, lakes and rivers, from drying up, is to guard them against wanton destruction.

Reckless deforestation and bush burning, or clearing of virgin land for agriculture and livestock, are among the water depleting practices that must be avoided; while tree planting and reforestation are to be encouraged.

Yet, is water availability all bliss, or is it, perhaps, a mixed blessing?

Too much of anything is harmful. In moderation, rain is useful and very much needed; but excessive rain causes floods, damages crops, takes lives, and renders many people homeless.

Like hurricanes and tornados, floods are a type of calamity that is hardly amenable to human control.

Another familiar destruction caused by rain water is soil erosion. While this could, in principle, though at high cost, be brought under human control, in practice soil erosion has, over centuries, reduced to barrenness large areas of what was originally fertile agricultural land.

Last but not least, water-borne diseases such as cholera take a heavy toll. It is estimated that some 5 million deaths a year are caused by polluted drinking water.

Therefore, vital as it certainly is for human life, water is not an unmitigated blessing.

CHAPTER IX: THE NATION'S BUILDING BLOCKS

1. Education

From time immemorial, education has always been regarded as a strong pillar of nation building. This truth is virtually universal, even though countries may differ in their approach to the subject, and in the educational content of what they teach.

In reality education is a life-long process, starting from childhood, through adulthood, to old age. Anyone who thinks that education begins when a child is enrolled in primary school, and ends when he is awarded a college degree, does not fully understand what education really is.

Education begins at home, literally with the mother. From the moment a child is born, his immediate requirements are first nutritional, and then educational. Good parents, and mothers especially – which is why a woman's own education is so important – provide this initial orientation as best they can.

By the time the infant reaches 4 years, he or she has already developed a strong sense of curiosity and a desire to learn, and the mind is fully prepared to receive formal school instruction.

Once in school, the child under the guidance of professional teachers, works his way upwards from year to year, climbing from grade to grade, his knowledge expanding, and his body and mind growing more and more towards maturity.

For a country's future development, the importance of a child's educational orientation during these early formative years cannot be over-stated.

Then comes <u>formal</u> education, which equips the child with sound knowledge of basic literacy–reading, writing, and arithmetic–before turning to specific subjects, and ultimately specializing on the ones in which he excels best.

Nothing is more beneficial, both to the individuals concerned and to the country at large, than the availability of a wide choice of professional disciplines. The freedom of choice inherent in the availability of such options is characteristic of a sound educational system, as can only be found in a free and democratic society.

Under such a system, a nation is able to identify, at a fairly early stage, those among its young citizens who possess special talents, to guide them towards constructive channels, and to reward them appropriately.

We may define this as the point at which the student–now a full grown adult–usually seeks paid employment, or starts a professional career; but not–emphatically not–the point at which his education ends.

Learned professors, including the highest academic award winners, and those at the cutting edge of science and technology, will tell you that there is still a great deal left to be learnt in their respective fields. Education has a beginning, but not an end.

Education may be construed, not as one building block or pillar, but as the entire foundation, of national development. Rooted in knowledge, reason, and understanding, and inspired by a search for the truth, education is pivotal to progress in literally every aspect of human life – social, cultural, political, economic, scientific and technological.

In essence, education is a liberator. It liberates people from poverty and ignorance, from witchcraft and superstition, from slavery and oppression; and it empowers all citizens – men, women, and children – to play a constructive role in determining the future of their own countries, and of the world at large.

Because education is such a noble profession, educators worldwide deserve to be held in the highest esteem.

But are they? Look at what is happening in Tanzania. Everyone recognizes the immense contribution to our country made by teachers, which makes the extremely meagre pensions paid to retired teachers an absolute scandal. Another shame – and this explains the 'brain drain' – is our failure to recognize educational talent among our own nationals, and to pay them the high remuneration required of their qualifications, and which are necessary to retain their services.

One regrettable, if perfectly understandable, consequence of our bad attitude has been a sharp drop in Tanzanian educational standards, and a tendency to regard paper qualifications, especially a college degree, as the symbol of educational achievement.

Cases of cheating in examinations, or presenting fake certificates, are on the increase. In Tanzania today, it is not uncommon to come across a 'degree holder' who cannot construct a grammatical sentence. Education is badly in need of rehabilitation!

2. Health and Nutrition

Next to education, health and nutrition are among the highest priorities a country must adopt in its nation building efforts. Failure to do this may mean that its best educational efforts are doomed to failure from the start.

'A healthy mind in a healthy body' is the most basic ingredient of human welfare. Body and mind are inseparable. While education caters primarily for the mind, health and nutrition cater primarily for the body. Between them, they equip a man with the basic tools for his welfare needs, and also with the ability to utilize them.

Health is more than just freedom from disease. It includes good nourishment, and the capacity to enjoy the pleasures of life, free from anxiety or stress.

Human health is a tender plant. It must be grown and nurtured, fed and protected. People need to be healthy at birth, and to stay healthy as they grow to maturity and beyond.

But man in society encounters all sorts of health problems, many from his natural environment, and some of his own making.

A well-planned health system must take into account two basic considerations: one, how to ensure that children are born and brought up in a healthy environment; and two, how to provide facilities for the society at large both for the prevention and the cure of diseases.

From these considerations, it is easy to see why and how health and education are two equally strong, and mutually supportive, pillars of nation building.

For example, if children are to be born and brought up in a healthy environment, a minimum level of education for the parents, and especially the mother, is absolutely essential. How can a parent be expected to have a proper understanding of the role of food and nutrition, or to know how to sustain a child's curiosity to learn, if she herself is not educated?

The development potential of a community composed of educated parents is second to none. Conversely, lack of education is one of the worst stumbling bocks on the path to national development.

Providing the facilities needed for health care and maintenance is a perennial challenge. There is no government on earth which does not recognize the need for good hospitals, clinics, and dispensaries.

But these facilities are expensive to build and to maintain, particularly in a country like Tanzania, which has so many competing claims on its meagre resources.

The prevailing situation underlines the need to choose priorities carefully– deciding not just what to do first, and what next, but also <u>how</u> to.

Take preventive care, for instance. This is equally if not more important than medical care. Prevention of common epidemics like cholera is perfectly within reach, if only the community, under the government, will spearhead a campaign to keep the environment clean.

There is absolutely no excuse for the constant overflow, during the rainy season, of sewage wastes into the streets and grass patches of a city like Dar es Salaam. Likewise, putting fruits, vegetables and other foodstuffs for sale on the ground, rather than on shopping shelves or market stalls, is a health hazard and must be prohibited.

If appropriate public health measures were adopted and enforced by city councils and municipalities throughout the country, that would have a marked impact on the reduction of epidemics.

Prevention is better than cure. A sick man who is treated and cured can never feel quite the same as he would have felt if he had not become sick in the first place.

Prevention is also better than cure for another reason: it is cheaper economically, certainly in the long run.

Even assuming that we had all the hospitals, the doctors, and the drugs we needed, and were miraculously able to save the lives of our epidemic patients, can you guess how much it would cost?

Believe it or not, preventive measures cannot cost the society anything as much as the enormous cost of waging a curative health war!

In the long run, not only is prevention better than cure; it is the only viable option for combating disease.

Nutrition may be counted as part and parcel of body building and health maintenance. It relies both on the availability of food, and on eating foods of the right kind, prepared the right way. Nutritional education and a proper understanding of dietary requirements play a big role in disease prevention.

Adherence to simple hygienic rules like keeping our habitats clean, breathing clean air, boiling drinking water, and choosing a balanced diet – these common practices, if adhered to, would go a long way towards building a strong and prosperous nation.

3. Infrastructure

The lack of adequate infrastructure is the first thing that hits the eye about a country's state of poverty. By the same token, the availability of good infrastructure facilities, in the cities as well as in the countryside, is the most evident manifestation that a country has attained a high degree of economic development.

Infrastructure facilities include roads, railways, bridges; building installations for ports, airports and railway stations; buildings and installations for schools, hospitals, hotels and recreation parks; plus sewers and drainage facilities, water supply systems; and information technology infrastructure. Strictly speaking, all manner of buildings, including commercial and residential buildings, are part of infrastructure.

These definitions capture the essence of the concept in its broadest sense.

Being a physical investment facility, an infrastructure item is therefore not a commodity for direct consumption. It only makes possible–or facilitates–the delivery of goods and services for human consumption. To put it differently, a major reason why certain goods and services are not accessible to consumers when and where they are needed, is because there are no infrastructural facilities to deliver them.

It is for this reason that economic production and the growth of infrastructure go hand in hand, and why the lack of infrastructure is one of the biggest inhibitors to economic growth.

For example, some areas of a country, blessed with good rains, may produce a bumper food crop, while other areas are facing crop failure due to drought. In the absence of good transport facilities to move food from the surplus to the deficit areas, food may lie rotting in one district, while people in another district are dying of starvation.

What is true of food is true of any other commodity. It is perfectly possible that the food deficit district had other products it could have exchanged for food, but was equally inhibited by lack of transport and communications facilities.

This example is enough to shed light on some of the development problems we face in Tanzania. The question is: why is the state of infrastructure in Tanzania so poor, and what can be done about it?

Whatever we may think, let us admit that in the end, it is positive action, and positive action alone, that will save the situation.

The pessimist will say that infrastructure is too expensive – to build, to repair and to maintain – for a poor country like Tanzania. Proponents of this view are victims of the vicious circle theory of poverty which, in the final analysis, maintains, tautologically, that 'we are poor because we are poor'.

What is needed is a change in mentality, which replaces the 'vicious circle of poverty' with the 'virtuous circle of growth and development'.

Turn the pages of history, and you will find that every country in the world, without exception, started off poor. But through hard work, persistence and determination, it broke out of the poverty 'trap'.

Then, step by step, it built its own foundation for sustainable development, one success leading to another. The virtuous circle of growth and development had begun – its building blocks being education, health, infrastructure, political stability, and a sense of self-confidence.

So, if others have done it, why not us?

Once we re-orient our thinking, the next thing we need is to avoid a common mistake: underrating the magnitude of the task.

At present, Tanzania has a population equal to that of California – some 37 million people. Ours is a very large country: its area, about 945,000 sq. km, is more than twice California's 424,000 sq. km. But–and here is the rub–the estimated per capita income of Tanzania is US$ 1,300 per annum, while that of California is US$25,000!

These figures speak volumes, and require no elaboration. They give a realistic picture of the task ahead if Tanzania is to catch up with the developed world.

Regrettably, even within the East African Community, Tanzania's economic performance unnecessarily lags behind that of Kenya, Uganda, and Rwanda. Moreover, the foreign exploitation of our mineral resources – with Tanzania retaining only 3 per cent of their value, and foreigners pocketing 97 per cent – is a scandal: in this sector, Tanzania is shamefully short-changed compared with, for instance, Botswana and Namibia.

Construction of infrastructure is a major development challenge. Of Tanzania's 124 airports (or air strips), 114 of them have yet to have their runways paved; and of the existing 79,000 kilometres of road, more than 72,000 kilometres are unpaved (to say nothing of many thousands of kilometres of new roads which remain to be built).

We must start work now, laying one brick at a time. We cannot wait until the day we are 'rich enough'. Development is a long journey but, as the Chinese say, even the longest journey begins with the first step.

4. Political Stability

Everyone, regardless of his profession, understands that development cannot take place, nor can its fruits be fully enjoyed, in an environment of political chaos.

As obstacles to development, natural disasters like droughts, floods, earthquakes and hurricanes, are bad enough. But, believe it or not, man-made disasters are worse.

War, terrorism, and oppression; and the activities of common criminals – thieves, murderers, rapists – all these can pose a grave threat to a country's political stability, and nullify its best development efforts.

Political stability, the source of peace and security, may therefore be regarded as an indispensable national building block, without which development of any sort will grind to a halt.

But while political stability is a necessary condition for national development, it is <u>not</u> a sufficient condition.

This is amply demonstrated by the case of Tanzania, a country which is a model of political stability, but whose development lags behind other countries in Africa and elsewhere which are known to be far less stable politically.

Tanzania's experience begs the question: what does political stability really mean? And how does its presence help – or its absence hinder – the national development process?

Consider two scenarios. First, a country may be stable in a *passive sense*, as under a dictatorial regime or a one-party state, where freedom of dissent is effectively curtailed: opposition parties are banned, freedom of the press is suppressed, and strikes by labour unions are outlawed.

The second scenario is that of political stability under a democratic regime –call it *dynamic stability* – which allows its citizens to enjoy all the democratic freedoms including the freedom to form political parties, labour strikes and public demonstrations, a free press, independent radio and television, and a free enterprise economy.

In my view, only dynamic stability under a democratic regime, and not passive stability under a dictatorship or one-party state, is a genuine building block for national development.

The political stability characteristic of Tanzania has largely been of the passive kind. Until recently, no opposition parties were allowed, there was little or no press freedom, no labour freedom, and most of the economy was under public ownership.

Political stability existed only because – and to the extent that – people had to 'toe the line' in conformity with the requirements of the regime.

It is not surprising that a whole generation of post-independence Tanzanians, from the early sixties to the mid-eighties, on whom passive stability had been imposed, was not able to build the foundation for growth and development that the nation required.

Tanzania's transition from a single-party to a multi-party system, and to a non-centralized economy, opened the door to new democratic freedoms, and new development prospects. One manifestation of this has been the privatization of public enterprises, which has been ongoing for more than a decade now.

Privatization is a step in the right direction. The fact that it has provided an opportunity for corrupt officials and politicians to enter into monstrous transactions is regrettable, but that cannot be blamed on privatization as such. You only have to wipe out corruption, and it is clear that privatization is the way to go.

The freedom of the media – press, radio and television – along with the freedom to form opposition parties, are further positive steps, which augur well for national development. It is erroneous to think that an opposition in parliament, or public rallies or protests against the government, are measures which automatically destabilize the country, or hold up development.

On the contrary, it is only when such measures are allowed free expression that genuine development, of a kind and in the direction that people want, can occur.

Recent events in Tanzania bear ample evidence to the plausibility of these remarks. As an obvious example: it is to the credit of opposition politicians, and of the free media, that the outrageous corruption scandals (EPA, Meremeta, Richmond, Buzwagi, Kiwira, etc.) have been mercilessly exposed.

Not long before, such revelations would have been impossible. In the name of 'political stability' (the passive kind) everything would have been hushed up, and nipped in the bud, by the top bosses: 'trouble makers' would have been silenced, irrespective of the risk that things might explode later on with far worse consequences!

As we are still in the thick of the crisis, we cannot quite predict what the final outcome will be. Some heads, no doubt, will roll; some properties will be confiscated; and some *'mafisadi'* fined and imprisoned; though a good many could escape with impunity: but who can predict what the final outcome will be?

Yet, regardless of their short term impact, these anti-corruption measures will, in the long run, contribute significantly to our national development efforts.

5. Law and Order

Last but not least in this series of presentations on the building blocks for national development, is the maintenance of law and order.

Just as education and health (earlier discussed) were found to be mutually supportive pillars of national development, so are the maintenance of law and order, and political stability mutually complementary national building blocks.

If individuals in society can disregard the law, and get away with it, a state of lawlessness will prevail, and the result will be political instability. Instability often leads to the enactment of repressive legislation, and in extreme cases to a declaration of emergency, at which point the nation's security needs inevitably take precedence over its development needs.

A national breakdown of law and order is therefore something to be avoided at all costs. Its root causes may lie in the physical torture or mental anguish suffered by the people, arising from political repression or other forms of social injustice, which cause people to lose confidence in, and rebel against, their own state machinery.

Our task is therefore twofold: firstly, how best to maintain law and order; and secondly, how best to restore it where it has broken down.

These are two facets of the same question, to which there is but one answer: that is, the country must ascertain that it has a genuinely democratic parliament, with laws which are fair and non-discriminatory, are well administered, and enforced by the courts without fear or favour.

The courts have but one noble mandate – to interpret the law, in letter and spirit. From the community's standpoint, there is little to choose between bad laws which are well enforced, and good laws which are badly enforced. Either way, the result is social frustration, a threat to political stability, and an obstacle to national development.

Our analysis suggests that political instability can be avoided if, and only if, the organs of the state – the legislature, the executive and the judiciary

– work together in harmony, honestly and with integrity, putting the national interest first. Such unity of purpose strengthens the spirit of community participation, which is a vital ingredient of success in the implementation of any national activity.

But, as we have already pointed out, national development requires, not just stability, but stability of the right kind; not passive stability but dynamic stability. There is a world of difference between the passive political stability of the type that was characteristic of Tanzania during its First Phase government, when political opposition was viewed as reactionary, or even unpatriotic, and political stability during the present (Fourth) Phase government, when opposition ought to be viewed as a dynamic and progressive force for national development.

Today, measures intended to weaken the opposition parties are regarded as obstructive of development, whereas measures aimed at strengthening the opposition are regarded as broadly supportive of national development. This is a fundamental change of attitude, which is clearly development-oriented.

Although internal political stability, of the dynamic kind, is crucial to the development of any country, external stability is also important. To be able to develop, and to enjoy the fruits of development, a country needs to be at peace, not only with itself, but with its neighbours and the wider world.

Nations which are under constant threat of external attack must earmark a large portion of their national budget for defense purposes, thereby lowering their development potential.

Some may call this 'a cloud with a silver lining'. They may point to the fact that military readiness against external attack forces a country to develop weapons technology which can have peaceful development applications. An extreme example of this is nuclear technology which has both military and peaceful applications.

In general, however, this argument does not hold water. The price of acquiring new technology the military way is far too high, both in financial terms and in human lives.

More importantly, any country whose external security is threatened tends to become a market outlet, if not a dumping ground, for the sale of weapons from various competing suppliers. This eats up a big chunk of its national resources, and may steep it in debt for years to come, without even improving its security situation.

The disadvantages of an external debt burden are well known: not only does it cut down the resources available for domestic development, but the external political pressure to which it the country is subjected is a threat to national independence, and often forces the indebted country to develop in a direction it did not want.

A country which is at peace with itself and its neighbours, which respects democracy and human rights, offers fair rewards to deserving citizens and metes out just punishment to criminals – such is a country in which law and order prevails, and where national development proceeds unhampered.

CHAPTER X: ASSORTED ARTICLES

1. Tanzania's Budget – Both Loud and Mute!

Of all parliamentary sessions, the budget session is the most important. That is why in any government the finance minister is a key figure, always close to the prime minister or president, and held in the highest esteem by his cabinet colleagues.

On budget day, the minister stands before the cameras, smiles, and holds high the attache case containing his budget 'secrets', moments before presenting them to parliament.

The budget is both an accounting instrument and a policy instrument. The accounting element consists of a review of past performance, particularly during the year just ending. Is programme implementation on track; or is it behind, or ahead, of schedule? For what reasons? What unforeseen problems – if any – arose during the preceding period?

Depending on the answers to the foregoing questions, the government will have decided whether new programmes should be launched, and which existing ones should be maintained, modified, or scrapped. This is the policy element.

Policy also takes cognisance of what is happening beyond the country's borders, as well as at the global level. In particular, the government must decide how to react to global forces beyond its control– such as fluctuations in foreign exchange rates, or in the price of oil.

Finally, there is the external financing element. To what extent is the budget dependent on external financing, in the form of loans or grants; and what external payment obligations must be met?

The entire menu of programme and policy decisions has revenue and expenditure implications. Deciding on expenditure priorities is the easy part. The core of the budgeting exercise is the revenue side: what new taxes must be levied; and what increases, decreases, abolitions, exemptions or other forms of tax restructuring are consistent with changes in government policy?

With respect to the 2008/2009 budget, how far were these norms observed?

The answer is: very well in some cases; but very poorly in others. The budget is both loud and mute!

In terms of broad priorities, the budget scores high. The proposed tax reductions on motor oils and the reduction in road licences are a welcome relief for transport operators and users alike. Priorities accorded to education, tourism and infrastructure are also about right. Agriculture, however, has been a bit downplayed, even if tax on oil for tractor engines has been abolished.

Increased taxes on cigarettes and on alcoholic drinks – especially hard liquor – are in order; and the tax increases on soft drinks can be condoned as an easy revenue catcher.

The budget may also be commended on having cut down donor dependence, if only to a slight extent. So far, so good: the budget is loud and clear.

Unfortunately, the budget is mute – and government policy therefore unclear – on ways to ensure efficiency in public spending. There was a time when this matter could be taken for granted. You only had to provide the revenue, and allocate it along pre-determined expenditure lines, and the rest was 'normal business.'

But this is no longer so. Experience has shown that raising the revenue needed and allocating it along expenditure lines is one thing; but ensuring that the funds are used as intended is quite another.

Nor is the problem simply how to avoid wasteful expenditure; it is also how to ensure that the funds are not stolen. In the absence of close vigilance, huge sums of money continue to be siphoned off illegally as private commissions, on faulty contracts, and inflated claims of various sorts.

The theft of public funds in Tanzania has reached alarming proportions. The past few months alone have witnessed big casualties in the form of ministerial resignations. Probe committees are still at work regarding the Bank of Tanzania's External Payments Account (EPA), and the Richmond scandals, and heads will continue to roll.

Considering the huge amounts involved, is it not strange that a key policy document like the finance minister's budget speech, and even the prime minister's, should remain silent on how the government intends to come to grips with the problem?

Surely, now is the time to establish a permanent, independent, judicial entity, subservient neither to the government nor to the ruling party, that can probe or pre-empt the occurrence of these repeated scandals.

I would also suggest that a well-trained team of lawyers and technocrats be created to oversee the negotiation of foreign contracts. No longer should the task be entrusted to individual ministries, departments or other public bodies.

The appointment of an <u>ad hoc</u> public commission to probe every corruption scandal has become fashionable. But the exercise is of limited value, if not futile, partly because the commissions are not really independent, and partly because their recommendations are seldom implemented. The exercise is increasingly becoming a tactic for buying time and diverting public attention.

2. Loans: Using Other People's Money

In the popular imagination, anyone who buys an expensive car, erects a multi-storey building, or starts a new factory, is a man with lots of money.

However, more often than not, it turns out that the man is just an ordinary fellow–an entrepreneur, with good business ideas and innovativeness. Otherwise he is probably no richer than the man next door.

The puzzle is a simple one. The 'rich' man will have borrowed money, that is, taken a loan from a bank or other credit institution. In other words, all he has done is to use other people's money to boost his own.

A bank loan is a legitimate credit instrument. It is not money laundered, stolen or obtained by false pretences; it is money which a bank lends at a profit to a client who is credit-worthy. That is what banking business is all about.

Borrowing from a bank is normal business practice. The transaction is a win-win deal, because it is beneficial to both sides.

The bank charges interest over a fixed repayment period. The client repays both the interest and the principal and, during the repayment period, provides the bank with some negotiable asset to hold as security, which the bank can sell to recoup its money, in the event that the client dies or defaults.

A major reason why progress in the field of commerce and industry in Tanzania has been so slow and hesitant has been the refusal to borrow, probably coupled with a reluctance to lend.

Moreover, people have not yet learned how to band together by forming companies which would make it easier for them to use other people's money – lawfully and for the common good. Instead, there is a tendency for people to go it alone, either individually, or in small family partnerships.

While kinship ties may be important for social and cultural purposes, they score poorly when it comes to success in business. Many family partnerships start off well, only to end up in disarray, largely due to the failure by the participants to draw a proper dividing line between business interests and private interests.

For example, it is hard to resist the temptation to dip into the earnings of the business to meet the financial needs of a sick relative or of one's own child who is facing dismissal from school for want of school fees. Yet, proper business ethics require that one should not yield to such temptations.

Better prospects lie in the emerging tendency to mobilise funds from the general public to finance public companies, especially those listed on the stock exchange. The laws governing the ownership and utilisation of the resources of a public corporation preclude the possibility of their being diverted to private use.

The nascent growth of the Dar es Salaam and Kampala stock exchanges is an encouraging sign for East Africa. The number of companies listed on their stock exchanges, their share price indices and their capitalization, are a good indicator of these countries' economic performance. Kenya's performance, incidentally, far outstrips that of the other members of the East African Community in this regard.

The ability to mobilize public resources, and to have ready access to financial loans, is a business culture that Tanzanians need to cultivate more aggressively. Good businessmen are those with the capacity not only to use other people's money, but to use other peoples' professional and technical competence, for their own business success.

Some nascent companies in Tanzania deserve to be congratulated for paving the way towards the emergence of such a culture. The best example is the recently listed National Investments Company Ltd which not only underscores the emergence of a sound business culture, but also empowers Tanzanians, including the small investor, to contribute to that development.

The banking sector provides a good illustration of how to prosper in business, using other people's money. Banks – even the biggest – do not have a penny of their own. All those billions of dollars or euros belong to, and are held in trust for, their customers.

A bank will collapse and go bankrupt the moment its customers lose confidence in it and run for their money. The fact that this rarely happens can be attributed to prudent managerial practices which banking professionals have learned, sometimes the hard way, over the centuries.

For the banking sector to contribute significantly to the country's prosperity, rigorous professional discipline, and high standards of honesty and integrity, are needed. The present proliferation of foreign banks in Tanzania is an attempt by foreigners to fill an existing vacuum – the lack of indigenous banking and credit institutions, with the necessary competence and integrity to attract and utilize local financial resources. The recent emergence of community banks (and of SACCOS) merits our whole-hearted support.

3. Our Membership of the East African Community

Tanzanians of the pre-independence generation, including all our former Presidents, as well as this writer, saw the rise and fall of the first East African Community, and are now witnessing the rise of the second East African Community. Have the member states learnt their lesson, or is history about to repeat itself? Surely, the new East African Community must not be allowed to be a mere carbon copy of the previous one.

With the benefit of hindsight, we should be able to sit back and take a sober look at what we are doing, or planning to do. We should not leap before we look!

Any country that voluntarily decides to be part of a wider community does so in order to reap certain benefits, or to avoid certain losses that would result from its exclusion. Each country has to balance for itself what it expects to benefit from membership against what it expects to lose as a non-member.

In the East African case, the benefits of membership seem to be the decisive factor. Possible loss due to non-membership appears minimal. This is demonstrated by the fact that at no time during the 25 years (1976-2000) when the East African Community lay dormant did any of the states, including Tanzania, feel the pinch. The Community was dead, and buried in a shallow grave. Nobody missed it particularly.

It is therefore not the negative or 'push' factors that are forcing us to join the Community, but the positive or 'pull' factors that are attracting us to it. It is our love to be in it, not our fear of being left out, that is the real magnet.

There is no mistaking the exuberant spirit behind what some regard as the creation of a new Community and others as the revival of the old one. By any standards, the march in that direction is impressive. Since the signing on 30th November 1999 of the treaty establishing the present East African Community, and its ratification on 7th July 2000, there is clear evidence of steady progress towards building a firm foundation for the ultimate goal of an East African Federation.

Burundi and Rwanda joined the Community on 1st July 2007, raising its membership to five, the original three being Kenya, Tanzania and Uganda. These five countries (three of which are land-locked) have a combined population of 120 million, and a GDP of $ 41 billion.

The Community is determined to establish a firm structural and institutional base. In addition to the East African Legislative Assembly, the East African Court of Justice, and the Community Secretariat – all situated at its present headquarters in Arusha, Tanzania – the Community is in process of establishing three principal economic pillars. They are: the Customs Union, (established since 2005); the Common Market, planned for 2010; and the Monetary Union, planned for 2012.

To expedite the economic integration process, the East African Community established, in August 2004, a "Committee on Fast Tracking East African Community Integration". The Committee has already made concrete proposals and established a firm time table for accelerating the process.

Some people have expressed fears at the very notion of 'fast-tracking'. They argue that this important edifice deserves to be built slowly, deliberately, minding every step, to avoid pitfalls. They cite the example of how long it took the European Union, despite its greater knowledge and experience, to come to fruition.

Building a strong Community is a learn-as-you-go exercise, subject to mutual trust and goodwill. Too many hard and fast rules, entrenched in treaties and protocols, could later become a source of friction.

An important contributory factor to the collapse of the first East African Community was tension due to the big imbalance in the distribution of industries between Kenya on the one hand, and the other partner states on the other. Most manufacturing industries were located in Kenya, while Uganda and Tanzania provided a duty-free outlet for Kenyan goods, with little or no reciprocity.

Moreover, the Community's headquarters, as well as the headquarters of several East African common services, including railways, airways, harbours, posts, telecommunications, and income and excise tax administration, were all located in Kenya – an unacceptable legacy of British colonialism.

Eventually, an attempt was made to rectify these imbalances by relocating some of the head offices to Uganda and Tanzania. The Community's Secretariat was moved to Arusha, posts and telecommunications to Kampala, and harbours to Dar es Salaam, while railways and airways remained in Nairobi.

Desirable as they were, these changes came a trifle too late. At best, they delayed the day of reckoning, but could not prevent the inevitable collapse of the first East African Community.

These events are still fresh in our minds. Let us see what lessons we can draw from them.

4. China, Tanzania co-operation

By a rare slip of the tongue, a British colonial governor, Sir Roy Wellensky, mocked co-operation between White-dominated Southern Rhodesia, and black-dominated Northern Rhodesia and Nyasaland, by calling it a "partnership between the horse and its rider".

Sir Roy had spilled the beans. His insult was enough to undermine what little spirit of co-operation existed within the short-lived Central African Federation, which soon split into three separate states – Zimbabwe, Zambia and Malawi.

Western countries try to hide their ulterior motives by saying that African countries are their development partners. Yet their trade and aid policies ensure, in effect, that Africa remains their perpetual underdog. Can theirs be called a genuine partnership, or is it a 'horse-and-rider partnership' *a la* Wellensky?

By contrast, China's co-operation with Africa is an entirely different matter. Even before the end of the Cold War, but more so afterwards, China's engagement in Africa reflects a genuine spirit of mutual co-operation.

To date, Tanzania is the largest beneficiary of Chinese aid in Africa. Co-operation between China and Tanzania dates back to the early years of independence. An exchange of state visits between Zhou Enlai and Julius Nyerere clinched Sino-Tanzanian friendship. President Nyerere himself visited China 13 times in his lifetime.

Probably the most important Chinese project is the 1860-kilometer-long Tanzania-Zambia Railway, which links Tanzania to land-locked Zambia. Built in the late 1960s, this vital transportation link was financed by a Chinese interest-free loan of US$680 million.

Other ventures include the Sino-Tanzanian Joint Shipping Co, Friendship Textiles, Kiwira Coal Mine, Mbarali Rice Farm, and the Mahonda Sugar Cane Factory; and more recently, new companies in pharmaceuticals, agriculture, and trucking.

The decline of some of the early ventures, established as public enterprises during the heyday of Tanzanian 'socialism', came in the wake of the collapse of many public enterprises due to mismanagement and corruption.

With the adoption of privatization by both countries, Sino-Tanzanian co-operation has seen a new dawn. Both Tanzania and the rest of Africa have much to learn from China's remarkable experience, which clearly demonstrates that privatization and Western capitalism are not identical.

Any genuine international co-operation – and China's certainly is – must be founded on the mutuality of benefit. And, if the relationship is meant to assist the weaker partner, the latter's share of the benefit must be proportionately larger.

Recognition of its one-China policy – which is not too much to ask – is the only condition that China publicly stipulates for any country wishing to co-operate with it.

China's co-operation terms are summed up in the 'Beijing Consensus', and those of the Western countries in the 'Washington Consensus' – both formally articulated after the Cold War.

The Beijing Consensus stipulates: (i) mutual respect for sovereignty and territorial integrity (includes recognition of the one-China policy) (ii) mutual non-aggression; (iii) non-interference in each other's internal affairs; (iv) equality and mutual benefit; and (v) peaceful co-existence.

The Washington Consensus stipulates: (i) fiscal discipline and elimination of deficits; (ii) redirection of public expenditure and reordering of government priorities; (iii) tax reform; (iv) flexible interest rates; (v) competitive exchange rates; (vi) trade liberalization; (vii) liberalization of foreign direct investment; (viii) privatization; (ix) deregulation; and (x) secure property rights.

China sticks to general policy principles, but the West propagates specific policies, and lays down rigorous requirements on how aid recipients should behave.

Aid recipients who do not toe the line are punished, by having further aid denied. There is no mutuality or reciprocity in this 'partnership', nothing that binds the Western donor countries to observe the same policies they stipulate for the recipient countries.

The asymmetry is stark. It is proof of the contempt in which Western donors hold their aid recipients, not only in Africa but across the globe.

With China, mutual interest is paramount. China rejects subjugation to the West, and has no wish subjugating its more disadvantaged partners.

China does not need – nor qualify for – World Bank, IMF, or other Western donor financial assistance. Despite that, China has made tremendous strides in its economic performance, giving the lie to Western capitalists. Once regarded as a sleeping giant, China is now held in the highest esteem, if not in awe, by friends and foes alike.

What lesson does this have for Tanzania and for Africa?

First, foreign aid does not hold the key to our development. Foreign aid can help, but that is all.

Second, we can and should choose our own priorities, free from donor pressure. On this, we and the Chinese see perfectly eye to eye.

Third, we are in dire need of relevant education and training, especially in science and technology, for the effective exploitation and utilization of our natural resources. A friendly donor, experienced in labour-intensive production techniques, is ideally what we need.

Fourth, investment in infrastructure, transport and communications, power generation and water supply – for all these and more, Tanzania needs an 'all-weather development partner' of which China is the perfect model.

5. The Sullivan Spirit: Building Bridges with Blacks in the Diaspora

Following the highly successful 8th Sullivan Summit held in Arusha in June 2008, a few observations are in order. Those who organized the event deserve to be warmly congratulated.

The spirit behind these summits is to cement cultural ties and beef up development efforts on the African continent, using the leverage of its more prosperous kith and kin in America and elsewhere in the diaspora.

A Sullivan summit is more than just a conference. Its unique value is the opportunity it provides for its foreign participants to brush shoulders with ordinary folk in their traditional African setting.

Seeing is believing. Impressions gathered from the literature, from the news media or from occasional contacts with Africans during their visits abroad is one thing. Perceptions gained from direct contacts with Africans in their home environment is something else.

The Sullivan summits have an impressive 18-year track record. The inaugural Summit was held in Abidjan, Ivory Coast, in 1991. The next six summits were convened, respectively, in Libreville (1993); Dakar (1995); Harare (1997); Accra (1999); Abuja (2003); and Abuja again (2006). The eighth summit, just ended in Arusha, has been billed "The Summit of a Lifetime".

The history of preceding Sullivan summits clearly indicates the high esteem in which they are held. Right from the start, the summits have attracted high-level participants – official state delegations, multilateral corporations, NGOs and private individuals.

Past summits are remembered for the various initiatives they launched over the years. The first summit succeeded in having $60 million of Sub-Saharan debt written off. The second launched the "Teachers for Africa" (TFA) programme, now managed by the International Foundation for Education and Self-help (IFESH) – a programme by which US teachers come to Africa to train educationists. The third adopted the "Schools for

Africa" programme, and the "SOS: Help the Children", which aim to build 1000 schools, and provide school supplies.

The fourth summit included an international trade exhibition, and focused on trade and investment promotion between Africa and the US; while the fifth concentrated on assistance to Africa in fighting HIV/AIDS.

The sixth summit held in Abuja in 2003 – the first since the death in 2001 of the Reverend Leon H. Sullivan – was honoured by the presence of President George W. Bush (his first visit to Africa), whose delegation included Secretary of State Colin Powell, and National Security Adviser, Dr. Condoleezza Rice.

Bush pledged $5 million for the TFA programme, and Chevron $5 million for the Sullivan Foundation. Agreements were also reached to build 100 housing units in Nigeria, to ship one million books to Africa, and to replicate open-heart surgery and other surgical procedures in Africa.

The seventh summit, convened in Abuja in 2006, also attracted high-profile participants, including former US President William J. Clinton, and ex-President of the World Bank, Paul Wolfowitz – plus ten Heads of State, 45 official delegations from Africa, the US and Europe, and NGO representatives. A million dollars worth of medical equipment and supplies were donated to Nigeria.

Nick-named the "Geneva of Africa", Arusha is only 50 kilometres away from Africa's highest mountain, Kilimanjaro, and is within driving distance of the world-famous Serengeti National Park, Ngorongoro Crater, and the Olduvai Gorge, the "cradle of humanity".

It was probably for these reasons that the 8th Summit chose tourism and infrastructure development as its main theme. Many participants visited these tourist attractions, as well as Zanzibar.

The 8th Sullivan Summit made one sensational path-breaking declaration: blacks in the diaspora, using modern DNA technology, can identify their linkages to specific African ethnic groups – easily, accurately and uniquely. This makes it easy for members of the diaspora to choose an African country as their second home, whenever dual citizenship is an option.

It could also lead to a great increase in the availability of human and financial resources, given that there are about 30 million Afro-Americans in the US, with financial investment resources worth $750 billion – more than twice the combined GDP of Africa!

One vital agenda item, in my view, remains: reparation payments owed to Africa by the descendants of American slave owners. The trans-Atlantic slave trade – that massive drain of able-bodied young adults from the continent which lasted for nearly 200 years – deprived Africa of its best human resources, and dealt a crippling blow to its development prospects from which Africa has never recovered.

Payment of reparations remains one of the pillars on which a Sullivan trans-Atlantic bridge must be built.

The presence of high-level US delegates at the Sullivan summits is a hopeful sign that America's attitude towards Africa is beginning to change.

Our hope is strengthened by the fact that for the first time ever an Afro-American has stepped into the White House. This cannot but augur well for the future. Now is the historic moment to begin deliberations.

6. Building for the Future

"Rome was not built in a day", so goes an old saying. Why did the ancients have to state this obvious truism?

This old saying is a standing reminder of what it takes to achieve development. It is not about Rome as such: it is about human civilization. Ancient Rome is cited only as a symbolic illustration of this great idea.

Consider a visit to New York, a city with which I am quite familiar. Looking at the infrastructure – roads, bridges, and building complexes – little or nothing seems to have changed over the past hundred years.

Clearly, those who, many years ago, built New York City, and similar cities around the world, did so knowing that it would benefit not just themselves, but future generations. Isn't that what civilization is all about?

As we build our own civilization, we in Tanzania must take a leaf from the experience of others. This does not mean making our cities a carbon copy of other cities. Yet, we would be foolhardy to try re-inventing the wheel, as if we had nothing to learn from the lessons of history.

Of those lessons, the single most important – based on human civilization the world over – is that no matter what we build, we should build with the future in mind.

If we look at the building and construction currently under way, or recently completed, in Dar es Salaam, what hits the eye is their sub-standard quality.

In and around Dar es Salaam, many hastily-built multi-storey buildings have sprung up like mushrooms, with some collapsing while still under construction. Can anyone guess what fate awaits these structures ten, twenty, or a hundred years from now?

Next, consider the roads. Here again, the situation is pathetic, not only in Dar es Salaam but across the country.

Peter E. Temu

An engineering contractor is awarded billions of money to build a stretch of tarmac road, but barely a year after the project is completed, potholes begin to appear and some stretches of the road begin to sag.

The source of the problem is not the shortage of funds, as is often alleged, but the unprofessional building standards, ultimately traceable to bribery and corruption.

Surely, if funds had not been available, the projects would not have been undertaken in the first place. No architect or engineer–unless he is corrupt –will do a shoddy job, which puts human life at risk and destroys his own professional reputation.

The whole thing smacks of corruption. Usually, the project supervisor–plus his bosses higher up–collude with the building contractor, who tempts them with an attractive commission. Having accepted the bribe, the supervisor no longer enforces the rigorous professional standards required of him. He now has the 'green light' to do sub-standard work, and knows that he will get away with it.

All forms of infrastructure – roads, bridges, buildings – are expensive both to build and to maintain. But maintenance costs will always be higher if repair work is delayed, and higher still if the initial construction was of sub-standard quality.

In the city of Dar es Salaam, the maintenance – or rather lack of maintenance – of feeder roads is something of a nightmare.

I recall an incident when a 'big shot' (Prime Minister Lowassa) happened to drive down one of these link roads (Shekilango Road), found it full of potholes, and ordered the municipality to repair it immediately. The municipality complied, to the great relief of the residents of the area as well as transit users.

In reality, the repair cost of many feeder roads in the city is puny, compared with the enormous social and economic benefits derived from them, or the damage caused by their continued state of disrepair.

Another illustrative example is Tunisia Road, which links the Kinondoni

Road and Ali Hassan Mwinyi traffic arteries. Barely 900 metres long, this little road segment has huge potholes, but carries extremely heavy traffic, which includes water and fuel tankers.

The road provides easy access to: a leading security company in the city, which is equipped with fire engines and ambulances; the only Heart Institute Hospital in Tanzania; and the much-celebrated Leaders Club. It is also one of the major approaches to Kinondoni Cemetery, where many distinguished Tanzanians have been laid to rest.

That the social and economic benefits of using this link road far outweigh the cost of repairing it is absolutely beyond question. Will the Kinondoni Municipality see fit to repair it, or must it wait for some big shot like the Prime Minister to order it to do so?

7. The Future Begins Today

For those who like using words with an exact meaning, the "future" is a vague concept. Perhaps that is why some people never use the word without a qualifying adjective – they talk of the immediate future, the near future, or the distant future; while others avoid using the term altogether.

Yet, viewed in its proper context, the future is a very meaningful concept. In order to remove ambiguity in the use of the term, I prefer to sharpen its definition: to me, the future is whatever lies in front of us, just as the past is whatever lies behind us.

In that sense, the future begins today. As the world turns, so is the future unfolding, ushered in by the march of time and events. Thus defined, the "future" becomes a more refined, operational concept.

In life, no two days are identical. With each passing day, something new unfolds – for better or for worse. We can see it, hear it, feel it; in short, experience it.

As we strive for a better life on this planet, we all try to turn experience to good account. In His infinite generosity, the Creator has endowed us, alone of all creatures, with the ability to learn, reason, understand and benefit from the lessons of history.

That is what enables us to face the future with confidence, empowering us to avoid pitfalls, confront challenges, and seize new opportunities.

The operational value of our refined concept of the future lies in the guidelines to action that it provides. These guidelines include -

First: Never wait for the future to arrive before you start work. The future is already here. Whatever you must do, do it now.

Second: Whatever your activity or occupational pursuit, do your best today and, by extension, apply the same rule to each succeeding day. That way, you automatically take care of the future, without consciously planning for it.

What we are saying, in effect, is, "Take care of the present, and the future will take care of itself." Does the idea sound reactionary? Does it suggest that people should give no thought for tomorrow? Far from it. The idea is, in fact, perfectly compatible with planning for the future.

The difference between those who focus on day to day performance and those who focus on planning for the future, is more apparent than real. The former use the more refined operational concept of the "future", whereas the latter, perhaps unconsciously, continue to use the vague concept of the "future" which we discarded at the outset.

Or look at it another way. It is common knowledge that for an individual, life is short and finite; it has a beginning and an end. A generation is easy to define: the period from grandfather to grandson, for instance, spans five generations; each generation lasts a lifetime – which is a finite period.

But for the community as a whole, the scenario is different. It is impossible to pinpoint where one generation ends and another begins. Preceding generations merge and fade imperceptibly into succeeding generations; and the biological processes of birth, death and reproduction ensure that human life at the community level is eternal. Individual humans are mortal, but humanity is immortal.

Once we recognise this, and reorient our thinking accordingly, we can readily appreciate that the betterment of the immortal community is what every member of society ought to be striving towards. That makes it imperative for us to be constructive and thorough in everything we do, knowing that each day, including today, is a small slice of the future we wish to build.

Economists, including myself, are known for agreeing to disagree. It may be hard to persuade an economic planner to stop visualising planning as falling into distinct phases of project design, implementation, monitoring, and review, each with its own discreet time period.

But one is bound to admit that this conventional practice underscores the failure to recognize that the future, beginning today, is a continuum which is not amenable to division into time compartments. Building for the future is moreover an all-embracing exercise, which ought to involve literally every individual in the community, right from day one.

This discussion is not meant to downplay the role of planning in charting our way to a better future. Its aim has been to emphasize a neglected dimension in the discussion: namely, that with or without any formal planning, every individual can contribute to a better future for the community if, day by day, he does his best at his own particular pursuit.

8. Road Accidents – An Avoidable Disaster

Road accidents in Tanzania are taking an <u>unnecessarily</u> heavy toll. I underline "unnecessarily" to emphasize that many of them are avoidable, and also to lament the fact that not enough is being done to prevent them or to punish the offenders.

News of recent traffic deaths of prominent people, including legislators, has been given wide coverage in the media. The list includes many other civilian deaths which occur daily, and are best known only to the victims' relatives, friends, and fellow workers.

The tragedy has five likely causes: bad road conditions; poor maintenance of vehicles; reckless driving; irresponsibility by the traffic police; and weak legislation and excessive leniency in its enforcement by the courts.

All these causes ultimately boil down to one cardinal defect in our society – the failure to take the matter seriously enough.

Firstly, our country has many poor roads, some with extremely dangerous stretches. Dirt roads, which wind and twist their way across mountainous terrains, or up and down steep valleys, are particularly risky during dusty winds in dry weather, or slippery mud in wet weather.
To avoid accidents, drivers must exercise great caution, and keep their vehicles in top mechanical condition.

Secondly, many vehicles, including passenger buses, in Tanzania are in a poor mechanical condition. Considering the extremely long upcountry journeys which they undertake daily over poor road terrain, it is absolutely imperative for the vehicles to be fully inspected and serviced before they begin each trip.

Unfortunately, few people take such routine precautions, with the result that a number of accidents occur due to tyre bursts, brake failures, and the like.

Thirdly, reckless driving is probably the single worst cause of traffic accidents in Tanzania. Reckless driving is totally inexcusable. Yet, we have to admit that the general public, and the government in particular, bear collective responsibility for this state of affairs.

These are cases of plain misconduct: drunken driving, ignoring traffic rules at stop signs and pedestrian crossings, exceeding speed limits, overtaking while negotiating a corner or over the brow of a hill, and, in general, driving in a spirit of competition with other motorists.

Good drivers, incidentally, do better than just observe the letter of the law. They show human courtesy and consideration for the safety of other road users and bystanders, including children and the handicapped.

What is badly needed is a sense of collective responsibility. The general public must rebuke – and the law severely punish – irresponsible behaviour by motorists. For certain traffic offences, fines are simply not enough: imprisonment and the permanent cancellation of the offenders' driving licences would be a more effective deterrent.

Fourthly, and regrettably, the traffic police are sometimes more part of the problem than part of the solution. In full view of a busload of passengers, a policeman will sometimes be seen accepting a bribe from a driver whose vehicle is either overloaded or has just narrowly escaped causing an accident.

Typically, passengers and onlookers either stay quiet, or look the other way. This culture of 'irresponsible tolerance' is shamefully common in Tanzania. It largely explains the continued arrogance, recklessness and discourtesy shown by drivers.

Cases where bus passengers rebuke their drivers for speeding or reckless overtaking are rare. More often, passengers, after narrowly escaping death, have been known to clap and cheer their driver for his daring and steering skills!

The traffic police must play a more positive role in enhancing road safety. This should include a careful and complete survey of the country's trunk roads, a demarcation of well-known danger zones, the installation of proper road signs, and tough – truly tough – action against violators.

Instead of always hiding somewhere near the roadside to catch speeding vehicles on their radar screens, the police should use their patrol cars to drive alongside the civilian traffic on the country's major roads.

Experience elsewhere demonstrates that this practice can be extremely valuable in reducing highway accidents. In the case of Tanzania, it would also enhance respect – and reduce fear and contempt – for the police in the public eye. A policeman will begin to be seen as 'one of us', instead of someone always to be dodged, or bribed.

Fifthly, why is the problem not going away? Are the traffic laws too weak, or is their enforcement by the police and the courts too lenient? Why is the public increasingly taking the law into its own hands?

In Dar es Salaam, if you see a man in the street running for his life, chased by an angry mob, the chances are, he has either been caught stealing, or else he is trying to escape from the scene of a traffic accident he may have caused.

Surely, there must be a better way to deal with suspected offenders!

9. Conferences: Expensive Talking Shops?

Do you want to know why so many people like to attend international conferences? Think of the travel comforts, the subsistence allowances, luxury hotel accommodations, sight-seeing opportunities, new acquaintanceships, and – for the accompanying spouses – the attractive shopping windows!

Regrettably, for some participants, the subject of the conference itself, let alone their contribution to it, is the last thing they think about.

International conferences – assemblies, meetings, seminars, workshops, symposia, call them what you like – come in all shapes and sizes.

Some conferences, like those which bring together research scientists, are absolutely vital: major scientific and technological breakthroughs, of Nobel prize fame, have often emanated from contributions at such conferences. Other conferences, including some high-level political gatherings, degenerate into mere talking shops. It is impossible to figure out what their accomplishments are.

At some high-level intergovernmental conferences, the spouses of some 'big shots', if not the participants themselves, have developed a tourism mentality, which regards these conferences simply as an opportunity for sightseeing, excitement, pleasure and relaxation – at public expense!

From the whole array of conferences, I have chosen intergovernmental gatherings as the focus of this presentation.

An intergovernmental conference is a public event financed, directly or indirectly, by taxpayers' money. To represent one's own country at such a conference is an honour and a privilege. A participant should never take the opportunity to pursue his or her own private interests at the expense of the conference's objectives.

Decisions as to who should be included in the national delegation, and who should lead it, are all- important. Equally important is adequate preparation regarding the position to be taken on various issues.

In the case of a ministerial conference, the minister leading the delegation needs expert advice, based on relevant information and factual analysis, prepared by senior public officials conversant with the subject.

Most ministerial sessions are normally preceded by technical preparatory meetings of officials who thrash out the agenda, and submit their report to the ministers. The report becomes a useful point of departure, if not the main document, for the ministers' deliberations.

If the conference is at Heads of State level, preparations proceed along similar lines, but go a step farther: the ministers themselves submit their report to the Heads of State, who use it at their discretion.

There has been growing concern that many of these conferences, for what they are worth, are costing the taxpayer too much money. Regular conferences convened annually or bi-annually tend to generate smaller mid-period conferences, as a follow-up to the implementation of 'plans of action' adopted at previous conferences.

Too many of these conferences have become institutionalized, with permanent secretariats, which prepare the reports of each conference, as well as the agenda and documentation for the next one. Thus, the number of conferences and mini-conferences has multiplied tremendously.

There is also a tendency to create committees, sub-committees, or working parties, to follow up on this or that specific item. The career professionals who staff the conference secretariats are never short of good reasons for convening yet another meeting as long as funds permit, or for making a good case for extra funding when necessary.

Conference secretariats have a vested interest in the continuation of the conferences they serve. They know that if the conference stops, and the secretariat is abolished, so too are their professional careers. This writer can vouch for that fact, having personally lost his job when the United Nations World Food Council, which used to organize ministerial conferences every two years, was abolished.

It should be made incumbent upon each conference secretariat to come up with proposals to cut down conference costs, or to ensure that they are kept strictly within prescribed limits.

Relevant cost-cutting considerations would include the venue of the conferences, their duration, the status of participants, and the size of delegations. Each of these should have a ceiling.

For example, it is believed that many conferences would accomplish just as much if certain countries reduced their delegations to half their present size. The staff of the conference secretariats should also avoid the temptation of multiplying meetings through the unnecessary creation of committees, sub-committees and working groups.

Greater advantage should be taken of the relatively new, but much underutilized, facility known as 'teleconferencing', a technique which could eliminate the need for – and the expense associated with – the extremely large number of mini-conferences.

10. The Politics and Economics of the Oil Crisis

Both the politics and the economics of the oil crisis have risen to a crescendo. This is the second oil crisis in recent history. The first was in 1973. Surely, now is the time to stop and think what these crises are all about.

What triggers them? What is their impact on both producers and consumers? How can we cope with their effects and after-effects? And, perhaps most important, what can the world do to avoid a recurrence of such crises in the future?

These are big questions, easier posed than answered. In the little space available, we can do little more than scratch the surface.

An unusually sharp rise in the price of a commodity may be triggered by supply shortages, or by a steep rise in demand, or both. Inevitably, where both forces are at work, the result is an even stronger price inflation.

Moreover, the general impact on the economy, especially on the poor, is greater where the commodity in question happens to be, as in the case of oil, an essential commodity.

Oil resources are not evenly distributed on the face of the earth. Some countries produce lots of oil, others very little, yet others none. In 2005, Saudi Arabia was the biggest world oil producer, followed by Russia and the United States.

An oil export cartel, known as the Organization of Petroleum Exporting Countries (OPEC), led by Saudi Arabia, the largest oil producer and exporter, was created in 1960. Its strength and impact were particularly felt in 1973 when the cartel, angered by American support of Israel in its war against the Arabs, decided to raise prices dramatically by withholding world supplies.

This supply-driven inflation of oil prices continued to be used as a weapon of war, attaining new heights during the Iranian revolution of 1979.

To meet the challenge, the Western industrialized countries, led by the

United States, while stepping up their own oil production and using more of their oil reserves, also tried increased use of other energy substitutes, such as nuclear energy, coal and gas, aimed at reducing their dependency on imported oil.

There is nothing unique about the current oil crisis. By a strange and most unfortunate coincidence, several factors have combined to push current oil prices to the ceiling. What we are witnessing now is *both* a supply-driven *and* a demand-driven inflation of oil prices.

The 'war against terror' which the Americans have been waging against Iraq and Afghanistan for the last six years has caused extensive disruption of oil supplies. Despite the overthrow and execution of Saddam Hussein in Iraq, and the defeat of the Taliban in Afghanistan, the end of terrorist attacks is nowhere in sight, and disruption of oil supplies continues unabated.

Military confrontation between Israel and Palestine has become endemic; as is the confrontation between the West against Iran and North Korea, on the nuclear arms issue. All this tension cannot augur well for an early end to the oil crisis.

Moreover, the steady upward trend in the global demand for oil, which even in normal times outstrips the supply, has now been greatly reinforced by a huge demand for oil due to the rapid growth of the two giant economies, China and India. This trend seems set to continue for the better part of the next half-century. It is hard to predict just when the current demand-driven price inflation will come to an end..

For a country at Tanzania's stage of development, the unprecedented rise in oil prices hits where it hurts most – people with the lowest incomes: rising prices of food, drinks, transport services, building and infrastructure.

Is there a way out of the problem? Admittedly, steps are already under way to step up oil exploration with a view to achieving domestic production. Yet, every time I think of Nigeria—which hit an oil bonanza years ago, but is still experiencing endless political tensions in the oil delta—I find myself wondering whether corruption and oil politics will ever, when our turn comes, spare Tanzania.

More serious attention must be given to the exploration of alternative sources of energy – such as coal, gas and solar energy. If the Brazilians can power their vehicles with fuel produced from sugar cane, shouldn't African countries, which lie in the same tropical zone, at least give the technique a try? Again, with much of Africa under the scorching sun, why can't solar energy be made a major alternative to petroleum fuel?

The point to realize is that it is in Africa's own interests to take these initiatives. Neither OPEC nor any other oil producer will support the development of competing sources of energy, for the simple reason that it is contrary to their own interests.

11. Is the World Financial Edifice About to Crumble?

The world is in financial turmoil. Will the financial edifice stand or crumble? And will African countries, including Tanzania, be able to weather the storm?

These questions cannot be answered on the basis of economic analysis alone. Speculation seems to be at the centre of the stage, and it is impossible to predict exactly how speculators behave from day to day.

Still, we can do better than just second-guess. Experience in the last fifty years or so has taught the world some important lessons from which we can draw, as we reflect on the opportunities and challenges that lie ahead.

What is the exact nature of the financial crisis? What triggered it? What is fuelling it, and how big is the danger that it might spread across the globe? Furthermore, is it amenable to control?

It is worth considering first the basic or underlying causes of the problem, before we turn to the aggravating factors.

The root cause of a financial crisis is the erosion of confidence between lender and borrower, due to the inability – or suspected inability – of a credit institution to honour its obligations. The problem assumes crisis proportions when the number of institutions involved is large, and their influence is substantial.

The current crisis was triggered off some months ago when a few giant corporations in the Unite States suddenly found themselves financially stranded: having incurring huge losses, they found themselves on the verge of bankruptcy, unable to meet their regular obligations, or to find a financial 'ally' to bail them out.

The resulting fear of recession, precipitated by bankruptcies and unemployment, created widespread panic throughout the economy. A heated political debate soon raged over whether to use tax payers' money to bail them out, or just to let them sink and die.

After an initial setback, the US Congress managed to pass a law authorising a bailout of US$700 billion for the beleaguered corporations. But while this may have saved them from imminent collapse, and temporarily restored a semblance of confidence and stability, the fear of recession continued to grip the American economy.

In this age of globalization Europe, given its close financial links with the United States, finds itself caught in a similar financial turmoil, and feels compelled to resort to similar bailout measures.

At the time of writing, with the crisis still looming, the US, Europe, and the rest of the industrialized world, in cooperation with the World Bank and the IMF, are teaming together to figure out how best to prevent the financial crisis from becoming a global catastrophe.

Every nation in the world is on the alert, ready to take pre-emptive steps to the extent possible, to 'insulate' itself from the crisis.

Given globalization, complete insulation is impossible, perhaps even undesirable. It is not as if the global network of banking and other financial institutions no longer serves any useful purpose.

Ideally, what countries need to do is shield themselves against the impact of the extreme volatility of prices in the stock markets, as well as in the foreign exchange markets.

Unfortunately, the behaviour of foreign currency speculators only makes a bad situation worse. Speculation feeds on itself. For the speculator, what counts is not so much what is happening now, but what may happen next; not how much stock prices have fallen, but how much further they might fall; not just how many companies may have filed for bankruptcy, but how many more might do so.

With the high volatility in currency exchanges that modern globalization makes possible, a speculator can make – or lose – millions of dollars, by just a few clicks on his computer keyboard.

Unfortunately this speculative activity, if uncontrolled, can have a far reaching adverse impact on the real economy. The free market will yield its purported benefits only if it is prudently regulated.

Tanzania, Africa, and the developing world, are at the receiving end of this crisis. Our import and export capacity is bound to be impaired by the activities of currency speculators who are presently hoarding dollars.

Together with Kenya and Uganda, Tanzania is already feeling the pinch. During the month of October 2008 alone, the value of our currency dropped from TSh. 1160 to TSh. 1310 to the US dollar. This makes our imports more expensive, and reduces the value of our exports.

This situation has prompted the Bank of Tanzania to declare that it will no longer sell dollars to speculators, but only to priority sectors such as oil, telecommunications and energy. It has also prohibited the commercial banks from lending cash for speculative purposes, including the purchase of newly floated IPOs.

Provided they take precautionary measures, Africa and the rest of the developing world are unlikely to suffer drastically, as banking and finance are still a relative small sector of their economies.

12. Put a Smile on a Child's Lips

At his moment of birth, a new baby cries out, not in protest, but as a way of announcing his entry into the world.

Thereafter, with his mother's tender love, the child is all smiles. He cries only when he is hungry, frightened, or feels pain or discomfort.

In his innocence, a child is an angel. His likes and dislikes are simple. He shares none of the common vices attributed to adults – ambition, hatred, pride, anger, greed, sex, cynicism, or the lust for power.

Keep a child smiling, and he will grow up to be a happy adult. And happiness breeds love, tolerance and understanding – the foundation stone for a constructive life.

If happiness is such a valuable investment, not only for the child's own future, but for the future of the community to which he belongs, it is worth reflecting what it takes to make a child happy.

It does not require much imagination to discover what puts a smile on a child's lips: give the child a delicious meal and a comfortable bed; protect him from harm or disease; give him the right education; let him have playmates, and playthings. Give these things to a child, plus parental love, and the smiles will come naturally.

Why, then, do so many of our children seem unhappy? What is it that wipes off, instead of putting on, a smile on their faces? For a short answer, one could simply cite the <u>absence</u> of the smile-inducing elements we have just stated.

But there is more to it than that. The way some of us treat our children leaves much to be desired. Too often, many of our children are not only unhappy, but even rebellious. As the following case illustrates, it is not the children but their peers who are to blame.

Consider the humiliating case of schoolchild pregnancies, which has become common in Tanzania.

It is bad enough when these pregnancies are the result of teenage school boys mating with teenage school girls. But it is monstrous when such a crime is committed by the teachers themselves, and occasionally even by a school head teacher!

I can hardly think of a penalty that is fully commensurate with the gravity of such an offence. The punishment ought to include instant dismissal, and an irrevocable cancellation of the teaching certificates of the teachers concerned.

Perhaps their names should also be pinned on public notice boards on a List of Shame!

Unfortunately, what is happening now is truly disgusting. A teacher sleeps with a school girl. If no pregnancy results, he easily gets away with it, and there is nothing to stop him from repeating the offence over and over again.

Apparently, no thought is given to the risk of HIV/AIDS infection and its grave consequences for the child's future. Only when the victim becomes pregnant, and her schooling is prematurely terminated, might the teacher try to appease her parents (especially if they happen to be poor), offering them a few thousand shillings, minced with apologies, and a plea that the case be not brought before the courts.

Regrettably, many parents seem to heed such pleas, which is exactly why these offences continue unabated. What they forget is that the future of their daughters and their daughters' children may have been permanently ruined.

Apart from the obvious harm of cutting short a young girl's education, childhood pregnancies are very dangerous to the physical health of the young mother.

The offending teachers must be roundly condemned because their behaviour is professionally unethical, and goes far to undermine universal educational standards. A student who yields to her teacher's sexual advances intuitively expects to pass the examination paper which is marked by her 'lover'. On the other hand, the student who rebuffs such advances knows that she cannot count on such favouritism.

Teachers who violate professional ethics breed an unhealthy mentality among their students. The grades, certificates, and academic 'qualifications' awarded by teachers in such circumstances are spurious and carry no credibility.

Might not this be the reason why educational standards in Tanzanian schools and colleges have declined sharply in recent years? Or why the incidence of forged certificates and examination leakages has become so rampant? Both are examples of how NOT to prepare our young people for a better future.

Regrettably, while most of us are striving to keep a smile on a child's lips, others are busy wiping it out. Government must see to it that those who are trying to build a better future for our children are protected, encouraged and rewarded; while those who are ruining their prospects for a better life are resisted and punished.

13. The City of Dar es Salaam and the Road Infrastructure

The City of Dar es Salaam currently has a population of around 4 million. Poor road infrastructure is one of its worst problems. As I write, I find myself thinking of a small patch of road, right in the middle of the city, that gets flooded regularly each year during the rains. The flooding is caused by something quite trivial – like an overflow of water due to a blocked drain, clogged with mud or discarded plastic bags.

Failure to unblock the drain, at a modest cost, renders an entire road impassable, at great mechanical cost to vehicles, and inconvenience to passengers, let alone public health hazard due to sewage contamination.

It is particularly frustrating when this occurs in the middle of a city with dense traffic. In Dar es Salaam, two of the best city roads, which carry heavy traffic – United Nations Road, and Bibi Titi Road – have small patches that experience precisely this kind of problem every time it rains, but the years come and go and the Municipality does nothing about it.

Potholes are even worse. They can be repaired at little cost, if the work is done early. But the more the work is delayed, the bigger the potholes become, the greater the damage to vehicles, the greater the nuisance to pedestrians, and the higher the ultimate cost of repairing them.

Another example of road neglect is street light failure.

To begin with, it is just a little thing: an electric fault caused, perhaps, by a vehicle which veered off the road and knocked down an electric pole. Street light failure may also be due to technical reasons such as faulty wiring or the use of defective electrical equipment.

Whatever the cause, the resulting black-out needs to be attended to promptly: no procrastination, no dilly-dallying. Otherwise, the damage will get worse, and the repair costs escalate.

Dar residents, like city dwellers anywhere, are always delighted to see new roads built, and existing ones widened and modernized, to cope with increasing traffic. Of late, such roads have included Ali Hassan Mwinyi Road, Nyerere Road, and Nelson Mandela Road, all of which are big traffic arteries built at great expense.

The scandal about them is the way in which their excellent street lighting facilities, installed recently and at great cost, are wantonly neglected by the city authorities.

On the day the projects were completed, our lighting standards seemed, for once, to match those of any street in London, Tokyo or New York.

But, guess what! Within a month or so, all the street lights were gone. The lamp posts, for which the road contractors had pocketed millions, were left standing – like ominous shadows in the middle of the street, stretching as far as the eye could see.

After being left unattended for nearly ten years, these "ghost" lamp posts have now become an eyesore. At night, Dar is dark. But the residents no longer talk about it. They tolerate it, willy-nilly.

"O, but this is typical of Tanzania! Good roads, yes, but little things like street lights, no!" This is the kind of caustic remark you will sometimes hear from a passing visitor.

All over the world, urban communities recognize that the maintenance, repair and rehabilitation of existing infrastructure are every bit as important, and more cost effective, than the creation of new infrastructure.

Dar must bring its infrastructure under close scrutiny. Beginning with the old areas of the city, such as Upanga, Ada Estate, Oyster Bay, Mikocheni, Masaki, and elsewhere, Dar should take care of all the little things whose persistent neglect over the years has rendered the city's infrastructure so decadent. The time for action is now.

14. 2009: Any New Year Resolutions?

If it were possible to re-live 2008, what would you do differently? The answer to that should be your 2009 New Year Resolution.

To the busy and mature individual, 365 days is not an awfully long time. Days come and go at the wink of an eyelid.

Each passing year has its ups and downs. A lot of good (and bad) events, some of them of a historic nature, can occur within a relatively short time span – a year, a month, even a week!

Whether good or bad, every event is an experience which has a lesson for us. Our aim should be to learn the lesson, and to apply it in shaping a better future for ourselves and our children.

Readers interested in a full account of last year's national events, and their implicit lessons, will no doubt find it in the pages of The Guardian and other newspaper and media outlets. In this short review, I will only touch on a few highlights.

The turn of the year saw several bigwigs behind bars or out on heavy bail pending hearings on official corruption charges. Regardless of the eventual outcome of the court hearings, this utterly humiliating experience, and the events that led to it, is an unforgettable lesson for all Tanzanians.

A resolution is a clear statement on what to do, or not to do. In 2009, our task should be to clean up the mess, once and for all. Our New Year resolution must be: 'Never Again!'

Recent experience has demonstrated the need for serious resolutions in a number of other areas.

First, there has been a tendency to appoint high-level investigation committees to probe major national scandals. The practice is to be commended. In the interest of justice, in-depth investigation is a necessity. The alternative would be to yield to mob justice.

I am reminded of an incident in which a medical doctor hit a pedestrian in a road accident. Out of compassion, the doctor got out of his car to help the victim. Instantly, an angry mob pounced on him and beat him to death. In the eyes of the mob, here was a big man driving a car, killing a poor man walking on foot!

If similar mob justice were allowed, the suspects in the corruption scandals would be shred to pieces by poor 'walalahoi', who cannot wait for the judicial process to run its course.

To avoid instant justice by the mob, therefore, investigation of all alleged crimes, including corruption scandals, is absolutely necessary. But that is not enough. Once an investigation is mandated, and duly carried out, people have a right to know exactly what its findings are. Its report, undoctored, must be made public, and not kept under wraps.

Moreover, the recommendations of the report must be implemented, unless there is a convincing reason, announced publicly, that makes further review necessary. Unfortunately, there have been numerous cases of investigations being undertaken without their reports being released to the public.

Even reports by commissions appointed to study important public issues – one recalls the Warioba Report, the Nyalali Report, and the Kisanga Report, among others – have tended to be released only reluctantly, belatedly, and in limited quantities; almost as if the general public had no right to see them.

Our New Year resolution is that this practice must change. In particular, all the reports from investigations already carried out, or still under way, regarding the current corruption scandals, including their judicial proceedings, must be published and distributed to the public, in a timely manner.

If this means that bigwigs must be paraded on the List of Shame, so be it! Social stigma alone is a far more powerful deterrent against future offences than fines and jail sentences.

Every time that some heinous crime rears its ugly head, our response should be to obliterate it mercilessly. A case in point concerns the albinos. These innocent citizens are being killed, dismembered, and their body parts sold to witch doctors who believe they will acquire instant wealth.

Our New Year resolution should be unequivocal: the government and the community at large should solemnly vow to respect and protect the human rights of albinos, and show zero tolerance to whoever tries to violate them.

We should take the same attitude towards – and severely punish – any form of witchcraft, for this is a plague to our national development. As with the corruption scams, so with the albinos, the general public is entitled to full information on how the scandals are eventually resolved.

In every case, nothing must be kept secret. We need to know the names of the culprits, and the punishment meted out to each of them. Not only must justice be done. It must be seen to be done.

THE END.

ABOUT THE AUTHOR.

Peter Eliezer Temu graduated in 1974 from the Food Research Institute of Stanford University, California, with a Ph D in the economics of agricultural marketing.

A national of Tanzania, Dr. Temu spent his first ten years (1963-1973) in teaching and research: first in Kenya, as Economics Tutor at the College of Social Studies, and then as Research Fellow at the Institute of Development Studies, University of Nairobi; and in Tanzania, as Director of the Economic Research Bureau, University of Dar es Salaam.

From 1974 to 1977 he served as National Planning Controller in the Tanzanian Ministry of Finance and Planning, and later as Director of the Institute of Finance Management in Dar es Salaam.

For over 19 years, from 1977 until his retirement in 1996, Dr. Temu worked for the United Nations in various capacities, devoting half his time to the United Nations Economic Commission for Africa (in Addis Ababa and Lusaka), and half to the United Nations World Food Council (in Rome and New York).

After retirement, writing books and articles became his main preoccupation.